THE MUSE

Nell Dunn

CORONET

First published in Great Britain in 2020 by Coronet
An Imprint of Hodder & Stoughton
An Hachette UK company

1

A CIP catalogue record for this title is
available from the British Library

Hardback ISBN 9781529327922
eBook ISBN 9781529327939

Typeset in Caecilia LT by Hewer Text UK Ltd, Edinburgh
Printed and bound in Great Britain by Clays Ltd, Elcograf S.p.A.

Hodder & Stoughton policy is to use papers that are
natural, renewable and recyclable products and made
from wood grown in sustainable forests. The logging and
manufacturing processes are expected to conform to the
environmental regulations of the country of origin.

Hodder & Stoughton Ltd
Carmelite House
50 Victoria Embankment
London EC4Y 0DZ

www.hodder.co.uk

THE MUSE

Works

Up the Junction
Poor Cow
I Want (with Adrian Henri)
Tear His Head Off His Shoulders
The Only Child
Grandmothers
My Silver Shoes

Plays

Steaming
Variety Night
The Little Heroine
Consequences
Babe XXX
Cancer Tales
Home Death

To Jem

SONNET 78

So oft have I invok'd thee for my Muse,
And found such fair assistance in my verse,
As every alien pen hath got my use,
And under thee their poesy disperse.
Thine eyes, that taught the dumb on high to sing,
And heavy ignorance aloft to fly,
Have added feathers to the learned's wing,
And given grace a double majesty.
Yet be most proud of that which I compile,
Whose influence is thine and born of thee:
In others' works thou dost but mend the style,
And arts with thy sweet graces graced be;
But thou art all my art and dost advance
As high as learning my rude ignorance.

Shakespeare

Preface

This is the story of a friendship. I met Josie in the 1960s and she became my Muse. I wrote two books and a play about her. My relationship with Josie was deeply connected with my work as a writer. Her use of language. The freedom and daring of her life.

I won prizes for it. I was pleased with the prizes. She did the living. I did the writing. She says, 'It is harder to live it than to write it.' (But I am not sure about this.)

And why did she need me? I was her audience. Her admirer. Her translator on to the stage and the page.

Her chitter! Her chatter! Floating around me! Lighting up my life!

Poor Cow (1967) was my first novel, which became a film, directed by Ken Loach. Josie also inspired my play, *Steaming*, which opened at the Theatre Royal, Stratford East in 1981 and transferred to the Comedy Theatre a year later. It won an Olivier Award, an Evening Standard Award and the Susan Smith Blackburn Prize before opening on Broadway in 1982, where, in spite of bad reviews, it won a Tony Award for Best Actress for Judith Ivey, who played Josie.

In 1984 it was made into a film, directed by Joseph Losey and starring Diana Dors, Vanessa Redgrave, Sarah Miles and Patti Love. Patricia Losey wrote the script.

The second book I wrote about Josie – *My Silver Shoes* – was also about her mother, Sissy.

Josie taught me not to think too much about tomorrow. 'It will come anyway and slap you down.' Meanwhile, there was life to be had. I would help her in the bar on the river boats if her friend, Joan, couldn't make it. 'Two vodka cocktails on ice.' 'Coming up!' And we'd stagger home, hanging on to one another up Putney Hill. Slipping and sliding on wet leaves in the early autumn gloom.

Cast

JOSIE

RAY, her husband

JOEY, their son

OLIVE, Josie's best friend

JOAN, good friend who worked the steamboats from Putney
    on summer nights

BILL, a South African man in a white suit

SISSY, Josie's mum

ARTHUR, Sissy's boyfriend

TEDDY, Sissy's younger man-friend

MARY, my mum

DAN, my partner

THE KIDS, my children

IVY and **MAY**, our Jack Russells

TONY, an older man, living in Spain

KIM, Joan's daughter, a potter, living in Antigua

NELL, me, the recipient of Josie's letters

Meeting Josie

I first met Josie in 1960. It had been a party night after Princess Margaret's wedding with the pubs open till late. I don't remember where I lost my shoes, but early in the morning I rode on the back of her brother's Lambretta barefoot. We were on the Roehampton Estate in south-west London.

And there she was!

Her dainty feet with small toes and nails painted bright red stuck out from fluffy pink slippers. It was chilly and she wrapped her arms around her chest to keep warm.

She reminded me of my mother, who had gone to live in San Francisco. She too was dainty (and wild).

Somehow Josie and I fell in with each other and saw each other most weeks. When I was with her I was a small child hanging on every word, entranced and enchanted. Sometimes she sang songs like 'Stand By Me'.

'When the moon is the only light we'll see.'

I shivered with pleasure.

Josie had married Ray when they were both sixteen and had a son they called Joey who was born when she was seventeen.

Ray was a bully and a tough man. He and Josie had been at

school together and he'd had to fight to win her and had to stay tough to get her everything she wanted. No easy task.

They had a caravan at Selsey Bill and sometimes (not very often because Ray wouldn't allow it) we went for the day or the night. It was nearly always raining. Sissy, her mother, would come too and bring her worries with her.

(Adapted from My Silver Shoes)

'I think I've got fleas. I felt something in my eyebrow. I'm sure I've got one in my eyebrow. It's biting me like hell. Have a look and see what you can see.'

Josie at the caravan

Josie had a look.

'Put your glasses on, Josie. I think I've got one round the back of my neck. There's something there. I can feel it itching.'

'There's nothing there, Mum.'

'Have a look on the top of my head.'

'That's your brain. It's where you've had your fall, it's affected your thinking. Your hair's lovely. I did it with the flea comb yesterday.'

'What makes it itch then?'

The rain stopped and we walked down to the sea and ate the egg sandwiches we'd made and drank the thermos of tea. I think at this time Ray was in prison so we could go to the caravan more often. And the children ran about in the wet sand.

Talking

We were at the caravan. Josie talked about her lovers. So we made a list.

Ron, Rob, Dave, Ray, Ronnie, Ron, Wolf, Johnie, Terry, Mick, George, Kennie, Jim, Bill, Blue Eyes, Israch, Rob, Paul, Deriki, Martin, Nigel, Tio Pepe, and a South African fellow. John, his name was, and he owned the Running Horse at Leatherhead.

He bought me a dress, she said. It was a white dress. A round neck, no sleeves, a small waist and a big green emerald sash and emerald flowers round it. I had white high heels and they fucking were high heels, with my spindly legs they looked wonderful.

And there were a few more but I can't remember their names, she said.

And I asked, Which ones did you love?

I loved them all – while I was with them.

We talked endlessly – about screaming and how the midwife slapped her face when Joey was born. Ray was away in Borstal.

How the room in Finborough Road had bed bugs in the

mattress and cockroaches under the wallpaper. She and the baby were covered in bites.

How she went down to the Cleansing Station and was painted all over with black tar to shoo off the bugs.

How she had to make the dinner in a Fray Bentos tin (eggs and bacon cooked in a Fray Bentos tin taste wonderful).

Josie had worked as a waitress aged thirteen (illegal) in Kensington Gardens Tea Room (now the Serpentine Gallery). Sissy, her mother, was head waitress.

Work was as necessary as breathing. All her life she worked.

And here she is!

From my 1966 Journal

....

We walked past the estate agent. We went in and she asked him if he had any flats.

She had this pink curler in the bottom of her ponytail. He touched it and said, 'You've left a curler in, honey!'

It was just the way he said it and he touched my hair, said Josie.

I do fancy him! And I'm going to have him.

Do you reckon I'll ever be happy? Do you reckon I'll ever get what I want?

Trouble is I don't really know what I want. What do I want, Nell? I couldn't really stick security for more than two weeks anyway.

....

It was 1966 and I wrote my first novel, *Poor Cow*, and I called her Joy.

This is what she looked like. Her blonde ponytail bought in Shepherd's Bush Market dangling over one shoulder. Her skinny legs and high-heeled elasticated black suede boots. Her little red mouth and milky blue eyes, her Cleopatra curls, her skimpy body with the large breasts.

She was always up to something. Asking for trouble.

Aunt Emma said:

'I warn you. Carry on like that and you'll end up like me with nothing. You can't afford to do what you want.'

Ken Loach was asked to direct a film of *Poor Cow*. So we worked together on the script. He was in charge of the structure and I was in charge of the dialogue. We both lived in west London so we could work at home.

He cast Carol White to play Josie and I introduced Ken and Carol to Josie and Carol caught her including the ponytail and the bony knees. It was a lovely summer. We were all friends and Carol and her two little boys moved nearby, to Putney. It was a happy time.

Publicity shot for the movie of my 1963 book, Up the Junction

From my 1966 Journal

We are walking up Putney High Street, me and Josie, and she sees a rack of bargain shoes across the road.

'Look, Nell!' she shrieks, dragging me around the cars. The shiny shoes like stars beckoning from the other side. She picks them off the rack. 'A pound! They're only a pound!'

She tosses off her black suede shoe, she hops about on one leg. She tries the blue suede with the satin bow slightly dusty. 'I'll soon rub 'em up!' Then she sees the red ones with plastic ankle straps, thin red cords round her small bony ankles.

'Which do you like best, Nell? Or shall I have 'em both?'

From my 1966 journal

....

Josie again!

I've got me rollers in me hair, a long nightgown, long pink socks, the top of a pair of pyjamas and he still wants to screw me!

Fancying men – it's what keeps me going – someone comes into the bar and his moustache catches your eye. You get a flutter even before you've touched them and it's like some magnet drawing you together. You fancy him and then he sees you and he fancies you and you're drinking lager and not feeling the strain – then he touches you – then he touches you quite casual like and that's it. You know you've got to have him if it kills you.

I need different men to satisfy my different moods.

....

On Saturdays we squashed into Joan's red Mini, Sissy too, and drove to the Arndale Centre, a shopping precinct in Wandsworth and there, after shopping, we would eat breakfast. Fried bread, tomatoes, mushrooms, fried eggs and bacon and then stagger back to the car and climb in, bags and coats and shopping on our laps and sing along to the radio. Joan was a skilful driver, dodging lorries and tipper trucks while I kept my eyes tight shut and hoped the drivers could see we were a car full of women singing along, making the most of being alive.

Joan was lanky and blonde with sticky-up hair and a ready wit. She had a daughter called Kim who was a potter with a business and a wooden shack in Antigua. Joan and Josie worked together in the bar on the boats that went up and down the Thames on summer evenings from Putney to Greenwich.

In the winter when the boats didn't run Joan worked in the late-night drinking club under the railway arches. She was saving up to fly to Antigua. If the red Mini was out of action, she strode home across Putney Common at three in the morning.

In conversation for my 1965 book, Talking to Women

Then there was Olive.

Olive

Olive was a prostitute and Josie's great friend. Sometimes Josie and I would visit her in Old Compton Street. We'd call up at her window and her head would pop out and up we'd go – there is a lot of boring empty time in a prostitute's life. Her maid – an old lady called Nell who had been wardrobe mistress at the Palace Theatre – would make us tea and biscuits.

Olive was a seductive, mysterious woman with a Mona Lisa smile.

Olive's mother was a spiritualist from Streatham. She had taught Olive to read palms.

The three of us would sometimes spend the afternoon in

my house drinking tea and chatting. Sometimes we would doze off and sometimes Olive would read our palms.

Then a post office worker fell so in love with Olive that he stole hundreds of pounds from the post office to give to her. He was caught but she had already spent the money.

Olive was beautiful. Josie and I thought she was the most beautiful woman we knew. We loved sitting about and chatting in the outer room. If a man arrived he disappeared with Olive into the private quarters.

'See you later, Nell . . .'

And we finished our biscuits and left.

And suddenly it was the seventies and I met Dan and we got together and a South African man called Bill appeared in Josie's life.

I only met Bill once.

He wore a white suit too tight for him. He had slicked black hair and smelled of a flowery, sweaty perfume.

I didn't trust him.

Next thing I knew Josie had run away with him. She never told me she was going.

Josie fell violently in love with Bill and fled with him to Australia on Christmas Day, leaving the turkey in the oven to burn.

Her son Joey missed her dreadfully. He didn't get on with Ray, his father, and went to live with his grandmother Sissy. He was fifteen.

During those years Josie and I wrote to each other.

Only two of my letters still exist, but I still have Josie's to me.

She didn't keep my letters because she didn't think a lot about the past. Life was all happening now and it was happening to her.

I have also included three letters from Olive.

Australia
1979

My Dear Nell

Well my love. I arrived here safe. God the plane was
sickly all those hours. I have now been here nearly a month
and am getting under the weather a bit I miss every body
and mostly Joey. I don't no how long I'll last out here as its
so lonley, but I'm going to try. Theres no one I can realy talk
to in facket there isnt any one.

I spoke to Ray on the phone and he was realy chocked so
was I. he wants me back but I'm tourn in half not noing
my head from my elbow.

Hope you and Dan are OK. Hope the kids are OK. Make
a go of it love. I no now its realy lonley on your own. and
worse still to be in a strange country. Anyway its all <u>fate</u>.

Nell Joey wants to come out here so I will ask you to go
to Australia house for his visa. if Ray asks you if you've
heard from me say no. Lets hope I'll make it. I dont no what
I'll do if I dont. I hope I'm stronge enough . . . Nell it is a
long way from home no one to run to now.

I'm hoping to get a job this week. I did go after one but
didn't get it. I dont feel myself Nell. No go. Funny in London

there was no stopping me may be I'll get back to 'Josie'. I feel a diffrent person; it must be because I'm another year older

Well my love I'll be closing now, look after yourself and the kids and most of all Dan. So happy you found him. Hang on to him tight! Your always be my dear friend for ever & ever.

Love from your mate
Josie xxxxxxxxx (Write SOON)
OR I'll be back. Give my love to every one
I wonder what the furtures has in stored for me and you too Love. I hope its all good.

God Bless.

Josie

IF you hear from Olive send her my love and put her new address in so I can write to her. You never no she might answer me.

I had met Dan in the 1950s when we were both students. He was over from America on a scholarship. We lost touch. Then in 1973 we met by chance in the street and became lovers and we took our seven children – three of mine and four of his – in the minibus wild camping in the Pyrenees; make or break a relationship. It made it.

Australia
1979

Dear Nell

Now next week dont forget to write No excuse for you, your a writer! We must keep intouch what ever happens. No you musnt let Ray no you wrote to me just incase. You dont no nothink you dint even no I was going. I miss my lovely house and the dogs and my family. I cryed many tears to fill an ocean. There no more left in me. I'm still getting <u>drunk</u>.

Oh Nell at the bottom of my letter I will tell you about Joey's passport etc he's had his injestions.

Ray was coming out here but they wouldnt let him poor sod over his prison record. I wonder what I would of done if he had of?

Nell weve only been here a couple of month we have got a lovely home. nothink to do with me. but its lovely, Bill bought it. He has so many credit cards you wouldn't believe it! !

I'll give you the address later. I want to ring you but I cant afford it so I have to reverse the call. I may have to one day but I no you won't mind will you? Its £3 for 4 mints.

Do you no Nell I wish I had educated my self now. I had the chance but never bothered. It would of come in handy now. I always did feel inferior aboat that. still who noe's I might start reading now and educate myself, every day passes you learn some think new. Who would ever think I would end up here, did you?

At this moment I wish I was sitting in your front-room. Yes I still get that frighting filling of insercurate why I shall never no. I awlays felt releved sitting in your chair. Sinking into it. I wonder how my little family are. I say my prays every night still. <u>OH NELL</u>. I wish I could run to you, Oh I'll have to go and do some washing or I'll be crying another ocean of tears it calms me down. I'll be glad when Bill comes in. Your right lonleyness is a terrible thing. I got a job in a club but Bill didn't like it. (Jelosee) So after a week I had to leave.

Well I've done my washing now. its 7/30 here at night. Do you no I never brought our photos of each other. how I forgot I'll never no. its very cold out here. I'll be glad when the summer comes. Christmas its 100c. My mum hoping to come with Arthur.

Well love thanks for taking my mum out for a drink. ring her up a couple of times please. There no more to tell you my love only I love you as a deer friend. write soon enclosing about Joey.

Give Olive my love. I miss her too.

I dont no Nell when I come home, I fill nothink. Life going pass but I no when the day comes I'll no my self. does that fill crazey to you? Anyway love write soon I'm just looking at the braslet you brought me. I need your confort so I'll close now. So All the best to you both and always good health to you and your family.

Until I here from you.

I'll be thinking of you.

And I'll be thinking of you too, darling.

Love Josie xxxx

P.S. Hope it is going O.K. with Dan? Let me know.

Joey was still miserable and wanted to join his mother. He was fifteen. Josie wrote to me again.

ABOAT Joey's VISA your have to get Joey round my mums to talk to him. He will have to go to Australia House with you take two photos and his passport and Vacnation Certifiet he has to collect a VISA form. You fill it in for him.

When the form filled in it has to go back to CANBERA HOUSE of the STRAND. NELL near Australia House. Tell him to leave every think with Canbera House. They will tell him when to collect it, when he gets it he's to take it round to my mum

Nell will you keep in touch with Quantas Arilines The Head office if you leave your phone No with them they will let you no when his ticket will be ready.

Anyway love, I'll be in touch but THANKS again.

All my love

Josie

I found one of my letters to Josie from the seventies in an old suitcase. It must have been written soon after I met Dan.

Dearest Josie

We went camping! First weekend away with no kids.

We drove up a dirt track by a river in Norfolk and parked the camper van.

I took off my clothes and slid into the green water. There were dragonflies dancing around my head and water weed in my hair.

Dan sat on the bank, smoking.

Later he fried cauliflower and garlic on the little stove.

It was the most delicious meal I had ever tasted.

Wish me luck, Josie. I am in love.

Xxxxx Nell

P.S. I miss you.

Malta
1979

I told Olive about Josie and she wrote, asking me to forward it to Josie in Australia.

Dear Nell and Josie

having a wonderful time in Malta, The Malta Feast has just finished, it was so Beutiful, I have never seen anything like it before in my life, there were people dancing in the street, and there were big Prossestions in the street, and at night every body gets dressed in their best clothes ready for the big feast, I wore a nice long dress, it was black from the waist, up to my neck, and from the waist down, it was nice and coulerful, with long flowing sleeves, with a long black sash round my waist, we were takeing photos of each, other, and of every body, and then there was the most butiful fire works, I have never seen anything quite like it.

Nell, I am still waiting for more photos to be developed, Then I will send them on to you,

Josie How is Australia? Please write!

hope you got my card. & letter, I will send some more, write soon, and look after yourself.

Much love
Olive
Xxxxxxxxx

P.S. Nell, *please send this on to Josie. I haven't got her address in Australia.*

Australia
1979

And then Josie wrote again.

Hallow Nell it was great to here from you. And thanks for sending on Olive's letter. And I'm so glad that you and Dan are doing well. Though I don't know how you could have swum in that river. Yes I miss you too and your always close to me, and I'm always talking about you.

I have loads to tell you mind you the first thing I must tell you is that the grass isn't greener on the other side. I miss everybody its hard making a new life Its very slow out here.

Nell I do so much want to make it. So I will have to leave it to fait now. But if anythink does go wronge I'll start again (You have to give me a kick thou) Yes I was so chocked when I spoke to Ray. I felt like running back, I felt so guilty because he been realy good to me in his own way, I'll always love him Nell no matter what ever happens. I <u>MEAN THAT</u> *I no he said he'll have me back no matter what I've done – but its my life.*

Oh by the way if you hear I took all his money Nell I <u>NEVER</u> *that's what Ray's been saying to everyone.*

Oh Nell I lost £1800 the Thursday before I came here. Stolen out of my bag. Fuck me. I need some luck. Still what it all aboat I'll start again. I no when I'm 50 I have plenty to talk aboat. (then I'm going round the world) Oh no I have to live with you and DAN. How will we all end up its like talking to you only my pen wont go quick enough.

Well Nell I'm working, it's for Rothmans. – as a reseptionst cant even spell it. Still get everythink Fucked up. Nice beige suit and if they promote me I get a car.

Well Nell Christmas is over and its nearly 1980 and I've been away a whole year. What ever does the future hold for us all. We met some nice people over Christmas. they realy made us welcome the ladys name was Bettsey. She gave me a small pice of good Luck stick which she got from a real witch dotor.

I'm realy glad you and Dan had a lovely holiday in the Camper Van and are the kids OK?

Dont you worry, I'm coming back to London but I want to go round Australia first.

Do you no what just flashed through my mind? remmber when we sat together and I told you what I will have one day (I hope so). well rember the white marble swimming pool and the cocktails and my emrald Green silk dress. I think I have that by the time I'm 40. 'Sexy Cow'. Bill brought me a lovely Blue Silk House coat. But I need the Patio and Cocktail to go with it.

Oh Nell and our first day at yogo do you still go? me falling asleep. No you kept snoring. and me fancing that bloke.

Do you think we've both found our match don't answer

that. lets hope we have. I wonder if we will see each other again? I do hope so Nell.

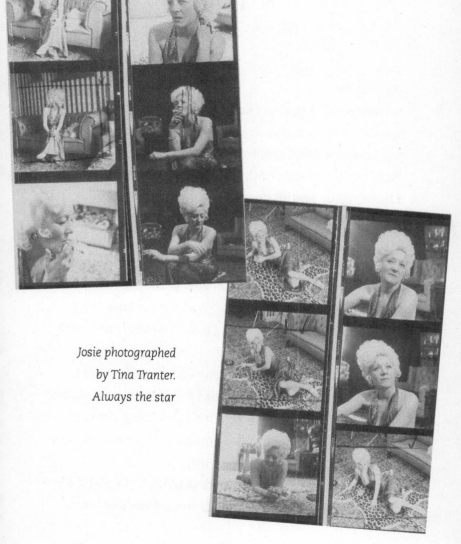

Josie photographed
by Tina Tranter.
Always the star

Australia
1980

My dear Nell

Hallow my love. Well I no I havent wrote but love I really havent felt up to it, you no what I mean. I felt realy up tight just latley. Well Nell thanks for those lovely pants. I was so choked and that lovly card. I havent wrote a letter for nearly a month I just cant sit down and give myself 5 mints.

Ray rang and said that Bill sold my car and my diamond ring and spent the money, well its just Fucked me up all together. Ray said Bill had put it in a friend's garage but sold it the day before we left England and never told me. When I confronted Bill he said, 'I sold the car Josie. we needed the money to get away. I was in trouble But I never touched the ring.'

Ray was asking if I would come back for a fort-night, but I had to tell him I was finished for <u>GOOD</u> and he wants it that way too. Joey finish with me too because I'm with Bill so all my pipe dreams have finished, I seemed to of lost myself, not noing which way to turn.

Bills working realy hard for me (REALY) but I fill I dont care. I dont enjoy nothink now. Its so hard making a new life Nell dont never try it. You see all you do is live in the past. I'm still working for Rothmans. Hows you and Dan I hope OK love? I do hope you make it with each other. I no you will.

Do you no Nell I just cant come back why I dont no, I just cant. I couldn't face it all, I try and get every think out of my mind but I cant Ive made a right fuck up but never mind. Somethink will become of it wont it?

Oh Fuck do I love him Nell or is it because I dont no nothink eles? I do hope every think works out OK.

Oh Nell I went to a girl baby christening in a spiritley Church and they got a message for me. I was coming back to London for Wedding Bells for me. Now what do you make of that?

I cant ring no more Nell as I have run a bill up over $1500 dollars. Ill be getting done for that next (Don't tell anyone). We have already had the Balifes round. Bill got me a Beatfull home and tried nocking them, so god noes what will happen. Still never mind I ask for it didnt I, everybody said he was no good but at least he treats me as a woman and not a skivvy.

Love to you always, take care of yourselves.

From your old friend (Bundle of trouble)

Josie xxxx

Xxxx

Then another letter arrived – from South Africa.

Nell – I had to stop the letter. Bill came in screaming, 'We're getting out of here now! Pack your bag!'

HE SAID Ray had got onto the police to report that Bill had stolen my car and then sold it. He was a wanted man. We couldn't take the plane because Bill would have been stopped. He had never told me he was running from Interpol.

That was Friday and I was half dead with fear and half the places we went through I don't remember. I had to let that job at Rothmans go and I loved it.

Fuck me, I was terrified. Again! We had to drive in an old banger from Melbourne to Perth. 40 degrees and NO A.C. So HOT we put dripping towels over our heads. And stopped at Petrol Stations to soak our clothes in cold water. I was crying. That night we slept in the car.

I don't want to get involved in Bill's thieving or I'll be deported. Will I lose Bill anyway?

I'm so mixed up! I don't want to be ordinary like everyone else (But I know deep down I am).

I wish you were here. I do miss our time together.

God Bless You Nell.

My love to Olive if you see her.

I miss her and keep you and Dan and the kids safe.

P.S. I think I am the one that needs keeping safe. I feel more dead than alive.

We got a plane from Perth. Singapore Airlines stopping everywhere and they made you get off – so you can never sleep. Sort of cargo plane. Cheap!

Love from your friend.

Josie

Xxxxxx

P.S. I'll write again when I have an address. At the moment staying with Bill's brother on the floor in Cape Town. Beautiful place.

Steaming
1980

Back home I was writing my play *Steaming* and I made Josie the star. I strung a clothes line across the room and hung bits of dialogue from coloured clothes pegs and made word patterns and invented dialogue.

The council was closing the Fulham Baths, a beautiful example of late Victorian architecture with original slipper baths and a place to wash clothes. *Steaming* is about a group of women who try to stop the baths being closed.

I knew the baths because for a while Sissy had worked there, helping to pull wet sheets and towels out of the washers and put them into the drying machines. Heavy work.

And perhaps by writing about Josie I felt close to her. She was in South Africa but she was with me. Saving Fulham Baths.

I remembered her saying things and hung them on the clothes line:

I've laid beside more pools than you've had hot dinners.

I may be skint but I've lived ... I can do what I feel like, that's something you'll never be able to do. If I want to go out and get drunk I go ... If I want to stay in bed in the morning I stay there – and if I want to screw I screw.

South Africa
1980

Dear Nell

Bill is in more trouble. Smuggling uncut diamonds I think and God knows what else.

Nell theres a lot of Which Craft over here and Devil Worshers. Remmber you told me one about that feeling you had aboat leaving your body thats another thing it frighten the life out of me.

That was stress, Josie. This had happened to me when I was frightened. It was a horrible feeling. It was such hard work re-entering my body.

Two men were fighting over me. (And I didn't want either of them.)

I'll be glad to get a letter from you. Oh Nell look after your-self. We wont end up on our own were always have each other, and our beatifull memorys. Tell Dan to look after you hes a nice fellow. Nell and you look after him. Do you here me?

Nell I dont no if my minds become a blank is as thou I

37

have no past. Its a very strange feeling. Do you no I dont feel guilty about leaving London like I did.

And now I'm in trouble because if they catch up with Bill, what will become of me, Nell? Bill introduced me to these people and I've got a house keepers job in a posh hotel. Its hard and boring. I hope to get something better soon

Love Josie

Sometimes when we had the money we would go off on holidays.

I lay in bed thinking of Josie and remembering Kenya and the good times.

The Safari

We had a huge tent with an outdoor shower. At night we could hear distant howling (and not-so-distant howling).

Josie loved it! And I thought about her love of life and I could so clearly see her sweet face.

It had been a last-minute madness.

And that meant escaping from our own lives for a week. Not easy to arrange – the kids.

Early in the morning we went out into the bush in a Land Rover. Our breakfast was in a wicker basket and we rode over hills and heard the roar of a lion and saw wild elephants drinking from the river. A white cloth was spread on the ground and we sat under a baobab tree and drank hot coffee from a thermos and ate bread and butter and marmalade sandwiches.

And the sun warmed us.

And the baobab is such a strange-looking tree. A scruffy tree, and careworn but beautiful in the early morning with the sun lighting the grey-green bark and the clean white cloth spread on the ground and the coffee thermos hanging from a knobbly branch and the sweet chatter from our two guides.

Josie chatted to the young men.

And I could bask in the sound of her voice.

I remembered something else outrageous she said I used in Steaming:

They're like stallions when they're young – fantastic to have it off with a young fellow if you're hot-blooded. If you fancy him – have him. And don't feel guilty about it – you've got to have a fling sometimes or you'll just get old and boring.

South Africa
1980

My dearest Nell

It was so nice to here from you and yes I remember Kenya and we rode on an elephant! I've got the photos at home. And Nell you always in my mind, and al the lovely things we done together. I miss you terrible and you dont no how.

I am trying hard not to get to deprest but some times failing. I'm still working in the hotel. I'm glad you and Dan are dong well. I realy am. I hope your both be happy. God noes what is in front for me. Nell dont tell my mum but I have given Ray the money from my savings account. Its no good, Money unless your happy. I no I'm a fool, but I cant hurt him no more. I rang him and we spoke for 2 hours.

Ray hates me being with Bill, he said he's been with some one eles took her on holiday but its not the same I am still the same to him infacked he said 'I love you more Josie'. there could never be no one else. he wants me to meet him half way in Sinapore just to make shore it realy finished between me and him. May be I have lost the one who realy loves me. I'll never no now. I have got to make it

41

now as I havent got nothink but whatever will be will be. (No I dont fill BRAVE just sorry for myself). And I still don't know if I love Bill. But I can't go with both Ray and Bill tearing me in two.

I'll be so glad when the sun comes its so depressing when its cold. I'm giving you the new address dont give it to no one and the Phone. its not my phone but its next door. Dont give it to no one. Well my love. I'll never forget you Nell in a million years. Your always be my <u>best Friend</u> and <u>truest</u>. So. Good Night and God Bless and keep you safe always & family.

Keep writing what ever you do or I'll die out here.

Love to you always

From your friend always

Josiexxxxxx

Steaming was going really slowly. I've always been a slow writer. Meanwhile Josie was in trouble.

Then she discovered Bill really *had* stolen her diamond ring like Ray said.

After the initial shock and heartbreak – and after taking his clothes including his white suit out of the wardrobe and down to the charity shop – she forgave him.

Then a hurried phone call.

'Did I tell you Bill was a mercenary in the Congo?'

'Be careful, Josie!'

It turned out that Bill was also wanted for extortion.

Oh, darling you worry me.

Why do you always throw caution to the winds?

Why not listen when I tell you to keep safe?

Sweetheart, take care!

The next day Josie wrote that:

Ray had wanted to come out and fetch me home but he couldn't get a visa again because of his prison record. I never told you, Nell, but he thretend me that's why I gave him all the money in my Savings Account.

P.S. Remember when we went to Rome for the weekend and you got drunk and nearly drowned me in the bath?

And I did remember:

ROME: A MEMORY

It was June and hot and we went to the Vatican and got trapped in miles of passages and felt a panic: no way out and hot hot hot. Finally made it back to the hotel all uphill.

Josie's legs had swollen hard and she was so hot. I ran a deep bath of cold water – a big deep bath – and somehow helped her in and she sank to the bottom and sighed with pleasure at the cold water. But how to get out?

I pulled and she shrieked and I pulled again and at last she was out and wrapped in a towel and cool.

It was such a deep bath I could have drowned her!

Next day we walked in the British Cemetery. How many young men and women had been brought to Rome hoping the sun would cure their tuberculosis? And Josie talked of grief, grief of friends dying and how would we ever manage without one another?

We wandered among the tombs and sat in the sun watching the wild cats chasing each other around the pyramid. I told Josie about Keats and Shelley (thereafter known as 'Your poets').

And then we went to Keats's house and saw the small bed he died in and how un-grand and modest it all was. How simple and true.

South Africa
1980

Well my love how's life been treating you; I seem to be telling you all my troubles as usal. Spoke to Ray, and he still wants me to come home and sort every think out, still wants me back but what tipe of life will I have although I would just love to see him once more, and Joey then I will have peace of mind, but if I went back he may not let me come back here. then I would go like a zombie

Its so frightning, as I am here I have nothink only Bill, and he trys so hard for me, realy I want the best of both worlds sicuritiy and Bill and I just dont no which one to reach out for. But I do so much love him even thou what hes done (stole my diamond ring and sold it), wonder if I'm being blinded by love. Can't see my way, you see I'm away from my responserblys so I blot them out of my mind. I just dont know whats right to stay or come home.

Bill doesn't want me to go to Singapore as Ray keeps asking. Bill loves me and think some think could happen to me and Ray wont let me come back. But I fill that I cant leave Bill because I love him, yet I want to come home,

Ray says go back to London when every think settled, then it will be safe. I just dont no what to say or do. may be if I do come back to London I could loose Bill and my adventure. Should I take that gamble? I took it when I went to Australia, but weve grown towards each other since we've been here. This is a thing I must decide for my self and cant.

Do you no Nell Bill has made me a woman? With Ray I was a skivvy. Do this! Do that! Realy but the way I think now is I cant go on with out Bill, I do love him but I cant think!

I seem to be cut of from everybody he trys to understand but I no he doesent. I'm getting that I'm forgetting what things are like who my friends and family are.

I'm to much round Bill and if anythink happened to him where would I go who could I go too. You see I cant leave Bill on his own, he needs me as much as I need him. I've taken on a completely different life, and I'm letting days go by instead of thinking of the future. I'm beginning to think to much now is it worth givin up every think and every body for one person cutting myself conpleatly off?

South Africa

1980

My dear Nell

Well love it was so nice to speek to you and Im so glad you and Dan are OK. and the children.

Nell I miss you as always but I'm still clos, not in body but in mind and sole.

Bill has started work in a car hire firm, He's not getting mixd up in any more crime. I'm pleased but miss him terrible of a day time.

I'm glad I came Nell or I would never have rested as you no. I no I'll find my rainbow, I try not to dream to much but as always my imaginashun run's away from me. I did get a job working in a Club with a Polish girl but we drank too much and they sacked us.

It so lovely and warm here, I'm going brown already.

I go for an interview to-morrow so lets hope I get it as a mangeress!

Love Josie

Never got the job. Gutted.

I, meanwhile, was struggling with *Steaming*.

I read loads of plays and dissected how they were made.

How many characters. How many scenes.

I was fascinated by the technical side. Actors getting on and off stage. How often they changed their costumes.

How long their speeches were.

I was discovering I really could write in Josie's language.

I knew how she thought and how she spoke.

Her letters brought her to me and I could tune in and imagine her chatting to one of the other characters in the play.

I could hear her cheerful voice. See her lively presence. I knew she was a long way away but she was here too.

Cheering me up. Making me laugh. Chasing away the blues.

South Africa
1981

Thomas Cook
CAPE TOWN
S. AFRICA

My dearest Nell,

Well my love how are things with you and Dan? I hope
you both had a nice Christmass and I wish you both all the
luck & happiness in the New Year and the kids. Well as you
can see I never came back home although I wanted to, but I
haven't got the courage. I no things will never change now
and I have got to make the most of it, and believe me I'll
have to try even harder. I fill now I don't care no more what
ever will be will be.

Well we have a furnished flat in a beatfull house the
house is lovely and some of the flats has black maids.
Funny Nell one of them came up to me and said 'MUMSEL
YOU NEED A MAID'. I laught to my self and thought I
could do with your job – I'm more broke than you!

So here I go again looking for another job! I try not to let it
get me down, but I no in the end it will, I keep saying it's a
long working holiday, but at the end whats going to happen?

49

Joey has deafinitly changed his mind. He is stopping with Ray. How long for I don't know.

Still one thing I've had my dream to travel. Nell S. Africa is realy lovely and the sun is beatful there are some lovely sights. You can see Table mountain oh its so lovely, and it has a layer of mist some times over it and it looks like a table cloth. The place where I live is very much like England, very old manor houses. I went to San serbastion. Oh I think it was called that where the first Dutch (African) settler setteled; he had a kind of carsel where he kept all the slaves until his home was built. Loads of antiques.

Oh we went to a safari Reserve. Oh it was lovely I'll send you some photos mind you I'm making it sound all honey belive me its not. but Im going to try and make the most of it.

I would so much like to see everyone its so lonley. Bill has been promoted he's now manager in Initial Car Hire so we have got a car. I wonder whats going to happen this year?

I miss you and Joan and Olive and my Mum and Joey.
Love Josie

Then a few days later:

Oh Nell! Good news. Bill has got me a job. He's now selling and hiring cars and I am After Sales Consultant which I kno fuck all about. So here I am washed and dressed and half the time not knowing where I am going.

I handle all the complaints – it is murder – they don't like this – they don't like that. I hav to write it all down and sometimes they say Ive written it down wrong. I say I kno what I'm talking about. I do it my way. Ive delt with your complaints. Now sign here! And they sign it good as gold.

I'm enclosing my card if you have any complains ring me.

Writing

Writing is hard. You have to keep your nerve. Often you read what you have written the day before and it seems like total rubbish. You fall into a deep gloom.

This was happening to me.

I'd never written a play before and had no idea it was so complicated.

All these characters having relationships with each other roamed around in my head. I had bits of dialogue hanging about everywhere. I didn't dare throw anything away and I was using scissors and Cow Gum to rearrange exchanges.

Often I felt like giving up.

But I wanted to show what Josie's life was like. What she was up against.

This is from my play, *Steaming*, 1981, set in London.

In the last six months I've been to eighteen interviews, I've lived from day to day like any dog or cat, driver, receptionist – they don't like my accent – sales rep . . . I've tried them all . . . what did I end up with – 'Radio Rentals', after taking half an hour on the 14 bus that never comes and sitting all day on me own in the back room answering the phone . . . if you think that sort of job gives you self-respect I'll tell you about last night when I goes for this job in the club. 'You've got such a beautiful skin, Josie, please take your clothes off.' Well, I thought, I may as well, so I've took me top off and I've sat there and he's touched me tits. 'What beautiful tits you've got!'

And then she said: I know I have beautiful tits. My lovers always told me I had beautiful tits.

From Olive

Olive and I both missed Josie. Sometimes we felt broken-hearted that we might never see her again. Olive wrote:

My Dear Nell,

How are you, you sounded so fed up and confused, and a bit sad on the phone? I will be back from Malta soon.

I really wish that I could be with you, or at least near you, I sometimes think that you are so lonely inside.

I sit in bed thinking about you a lot, wishing I was there to really make you laugh, Because we have both had laughs, and cheard each other up, it really makes me feel sad, when I think of you that way, sometimes I think that when you are nice and kind and talk to people who come to see you, and sometimes you laugh.

I feel you don't really want to. But you do even if it's just to be sociable. But I'm sure your crying and sad inside for some reason. Nell, I really love you, you are the only person that I've ever met in my life, to be such a true friend, if ever you needed me for any reason I would drop everything and come to you, you mean so much to me, I love telling you about the things I get up to, I know that one day we will do something so funny together, and we will laugh for the rest of our Live's. Oh well I will finish now to catch the Post. So don't forget think of the good times.

oh, by the way Nell I Phoned Josie she was so happy to hear from me. She wanted to come and see me in hospital before she left but she never made it. The next day she ran away with Bill.

Nell Love I must finish now, Look After yourself won't you, don't let people get on top of you, speak your mind. Just think free and be yourself and do your own thing. Kiss the kids for me.

Lot's of love from your real friend Olive

I will come and see you as soon as I'm back.

Xxxxxxxxxxxxxxxxxx

Dearest Olive

It is 3.30 in the morning and I am awake and thinking of you.

Do you remember when you were staying with me a long time ago (and before I had met Dan)?

And you came back to my house with a plastic bag full of ten pound notes and I was in bed asleep and you scattered the notes all over me and they went everywhere and we spent an hour collecting them back up and it began to get light and it was a new day.

Now here I am without you. Please take care of yourself. So many thoughts and memories, dear Olive.

Love

Nell

P.S. Perhaps we will follow Joan to Antigua and stay with her in Kim's wooden hut and walk barefoot in the warm sand?

It would do us good.

Sometimes I go down. Really down – slump, plunge, fall, shatter, close up, close down and disappear.

Olive had seen me through some sharp plunges. Held my hand and pulled me up to the surface.

Whatever was happening to her she had time for what was happening to me.

South Africa
1981

Nell love I've just got your letter Oh love I was so pleased
your never no, Nell love I miss you but as long as we write
to each other were still feel close, as always.

Nell Nell the sun is still shinning on me, and I feel happy.
I hope it last, Bill and I feel more in love than we ever
thought, Oh Nell its like a new life I'm not going to think of
it every ending I hope it last for ever & ever.

I was so pleased my phone call came at the right time,
as you can always make me feel good and at ease. And my
job as After Sales Consultant is going ok. I'm hanging in
there.

As I said Bill is at work, still manager of Initial Cars
realy trying for us both and I have now got lots of faith in
him he's going to make it. I no he will, he promised, but if
he doesn't I wont condem him it will only be because hes
weak, and we all have weakness don't we love?

But he makes me feel good hes like food to me, air, blood.
So all I can give him is my love and myself, and thats
enough. No I dont think, were be in anymore trouble hes
getting to old for that.

I think Nell, we leane on each other, we are misfit so we can dream together live in our own world.

Nell I have a confestom to make, I went to the swimming pool with this young girl. Well one of her friends was a fellow I fancied. I was walken along with him and there was Bill at the door of the hotel. Well my heart went in my mouth. He thought all the wronge way. His face went black. There were sparks coming out of his eyes.

When I got home he was fuming. I tried to explain. He wouldn't lissen. So he went off and would not take me. So off I went YES! With the young girl and the bloke I went on from the pool to all the clubs and I got drunk anyway, had a terrific time cant remember much, but it was lovely and I let my self go and I danced half the night.

Next day

Your letter came I feel happy again and to no Joey OK I feel happy. Yes the sun is shinning. But Bill is away at work so here I am on my own again but Nell I dont no if this is what I want?

Now lisen to what happen. Saturday the puff Charles had a drink we went along and we chatted aload of shit anyway as the time went on it got worse. His mother got drunk, he went for her shook her and started on her. I snaped and went for him with a bottle I dont no what got into me. but that class I dont need them.

Bill is so jealous Nell. Now he's at work I can tell you what happen. I did get off with that Block at the pool. He was American lovely & tasty and Saturday night I was with an Irish fellow 23. It was lovely. I need excitement. Dont mention this in your next letter in case he reads it.

I feel turned on by the whole lot of it. But Bill wont stand it He said I cant drink no more only with him.

Bill still turn me on too. I think its because I no he loves me now and I want to be wicked to him. I want to have my flirtation and him at the same time. I still want the best of both worlds and I'm going to have them while it lasts.

And as for you and Dan dont hurt him, make beautiful love, I miss you Nell I wish you was here to tell you more.

Bill is away more because he has steped into a new job at Towel Master – 800 Rand a month!. I don't realy have to go to work,

Hes not to bad, realy but I think he loves me more than I do him, if I look at anyone he still goes mad. So I do it all the more.

No he said your mine. He think I gone wild, he said. You're all woman he said so that made me feel nice Vain A'?. I know I look very well at the moment. So he IS good for me.

Well my darling hope you got my last letter. now be happy. yes I still have that monster inside me. It's like a hunger for something I never quite get. So when I come home I hope its gone.

Thank for telling me about Joey. Tell him you heard from me. I write later to him. Best he stays with Ray.

Be happy Nell. Hows your mum? How's the play going? I wish I were with you.

Darling no one can have friendship like ours. Write soon 'Promise'.

Love to Dan. Tell him Life not so bad, Cuddle him up tonight and give him plenty of loving

God Bless always

Keep warm

Love from

Josie xxxxxx

Xxxx

Wrote and told Josie that my mum had married her American sports writer who drank.

'*Good for her!*' wrote Josie.

But it wasn't.

Turned out to be a very bad idea. (He was violent.) And I had to help her escape. Josie had met my mother a couple of times in my house and they had really taken to each other. Both had agreed life was something you never got under control. And that perhaps there was no point in trying.

'Have fun, darling.' (Mum!)

A line from Josie that I put into *Steaming*:

'*I've got to have excitement or I die.*'

South Africa
1981

My dear Nell

Just these few lines to say thanks for your lovely letter.

Nell I can imagin the beautiful bathroom suits at Harrods. Lets have a blood red one with Gold taps 'Cupide' white silk curtains. White carpet. We will have to bath each other. Now my love I'm inclosing a cheque can you cash it and send it on as those phone calls caught up. Bill paying ½ I'm paying the other.

Well to-day we went to a lovely river and we sat by it and you could here the water running down into the rocks. It was beautiful it made me think of you I was going to write there but it was so hot. I'll make you jealose well I'm going brown. Well if all goes well I start work part time with Bill Tuesday. As I say Bill's steped into a better job SALES MANAGER so I'll be under him at Towel Master. Mind you he's got to come home so he's got no chance to boss me.

Bill's coming along fine. I hope we stay happy. but nowing me. who noes.

How are you and Dan? send him my love.

Well love hope the kids are OK, Nell I do miss you although I have Bill I do miss you its not the same. he doesn't under-stand me like you do. I'll never have a friend like you.

I wish we could live over there so then we would both have what we want. Nell one day we will be together I NO. And so do you even if its only in heaven. thats what you mean to me. so when you feel lonely, just think, I think of you often.

Well my love I be closing now. So chin up keep writing and loving.

Write soon, every week.

Love to you always. And good luck with 'Steaming'.

From Your friend for ever

Josie

Xxxxx

P.S. Joan coming soon. Tell her not to say nothing about the clothes in front of Bill. Did I tell you I gave them to the charity shop? Including The White Suit. It was too tight anyway. I was in such a temper when I heard he'd sold my car AND my diamond ring. He still deosn't kno what happened to them. Thinks they were stolen from the wardrobe.

Joan is really excited.

She saved up for the ticket working late plus she sold the red Mini.

Josie by the river

South Africa
1981

Joan visits Josie

Joan was a brilliant traveller. One of those who goes with just a knapsack and sleeps through the whole flight. She'd work late hours behind the bar on the boats. Earn and spend, earn and spend, that was Joan's philosophy.

My dear Nell,

Well love Joan got here safe. I was so pleased to see her. We both cried when we saw each other.

Sorry I haven't written for so long but I was busy with Joan. Took her everywhere! She loved it!

She got on Bill's nerves a bit (talks too much).

We went dancing in The Gold Frog, got drunk twice.

Went to the beach. I miss her. She will tell you all about it.

Love Josie

Do you remember one summer night I came on the river boat with you and Joan? I took the downstairs bar with you pulling pints – bloody hard work! – and Joan was upstairs on deck with the cocktails (her speciality). Two Bloody Marys coming up! (Plenty of ice then you didn't need to put so much vodka in.) And then Joanie would turn on the music and dance. She was tall and strong and an amazing dancer and Josie would abandon the tea urn and snuck upstairs and together they'd dance. Strong, tall Joan would sling dainty, light Josie over her shoulder and spin her like a top. The delighted punters would gather to watch and clap in time to the music. Those nights!

South Africa
1981

My dear Nell

*Nell by now you will of seen Joan and herd all aboat
South Africa. good things has happened to me So I'll enjoy
as much as I can while I'm here. I swam for the first time
Sunday. Really nearly 1 length but I had my rubber ring on.
I'll send photos of me. It was the day Joan left and she was
really happy that I could swim and she had taught me!
(She said not to hurry to get out of the rubber ring.)*

*Bill is still at work at Towel Master, late as usal, flogging
himself to death, it worries me thou. He is trying to go straight
and be a good earner. Hard! I wish some think nice would
happen lifes very borring at the moment. I crave excitement.*

*Nell love I got your lovely letter today I have just got
back from the dentis and I had that injection Metherdrine?
I think its called that and it feels lovely. As I've had all my
teeth done now thank God you no what a coward I am. Do
you like my posh letter paper, pretty is it well love I wont
be sending this letter of strate away as there one in the
post but I'll still keep writing it then.*

I hate a rotine now day in day out the same. I no I shouldn't be grumberling but I am. Shall I tell you my fantsy at the moment to be wearing a beautiful silk dress white. looking good, having cocktail on a Miami beach, how does that sound?

Sounds good, Josie.

Dont need a man. I fed up with men, there not worth the trouble.

I decided I dont need the heart acks. I dont want to end up with nothing it frightens me Nell it realy does. So I must face every day as it comes. You see Nell it 10 to 6 and I'm all alone no one to talk to while Bill is working late .

But my time is coming I'll just pack up and go. I want to try and get my fare myself then Ive acheaved some think. do you under-stand what I mean?

Bill's frighten Because hes relized whats life all aboat and he has nothink.

Maybe he'll make it who no, but maybe I cant wait around to find out. (Aren't I wicked).

Well love I decide to put this letter in with the other one as its still in my brief cass.

I wish you was here, to talk to, just to smile to feel alive again Nell I musnt get morbed must I? Or I'll let Women's Lib down.

Nell I have to close now Nell as I will get up tight.

See you love write Soon

always be happy.

Love

Josie xxxx

South Africa
1981

My dear Nell

Nell love nearly another month over to-day I feel a bit under the weather. Oh Nell. I feel so lost, and demoralised. I no I must not feel sorry for myself but I do. What's going to happen to me?

Some think happen the other night. When I tell you your laugh but cry.

It all started like this Bill and myself went to one of his reps house. Oh it was such a beautiful house right up in a mountain Oh it was out of this world. She about 43. We had a drink. 'Scotch'. I got the tast. Anyway on the way home we stoped in for another one. Then the rain came and lightening. so when we got home we went to the top of the flats to the roof up 23 floors to watch the storm and he wanted to make love but Nell I was freazing anyway. Wwe had an armament so I walked down 23 floors. Bill took the lift. When I reach our flat I was so in a temper. I went for him, he called me every name in the book. then I went to bed I was still screaming and shouting, so he put his hand over my mouth, and scratched my face, so I waited till he was asleep. I boiled the kettle, and pawed it over him. Well all of a sudden he came to the kitchen, with his belt. god. Did he give it to me. my body stun. I couldnt belive it. well I was going to get on the first plane back. that was my idea. I didn't do it. anyway then he went back to bed. Next morning I was so chocked, I thought of so many things. I no I shouldn't of done it. But fancy him doing that! He said if you want to do bad things then you must be punished. Well I have had to stay in for 2 days, my legs feel like growing pains but I think thats all those stair.

Oh he wants me to marry him then he'll feel better. But I have to tell you, the truth, I dont no if I do love Bill. may be its because he pays a lot of atention to me, I need Bill at the moment. God Nell I think I need a sarcatrish? I'll feel very strange alone. Nell, hes good to me. I cant say hes not and I wont starve.

Anyway now thanks to Towel Master hes gone after a house with a swimming pool. I hope he gets it its only rented, he said if He can make me have sercurty I would sort myself out.

Do you think he loves me? Oh he said he's never expernced a person like me, hes never been in love like this, Oh anyway leave it to the future.

Nell I dont no if I've done the right thing or wronge.

But this time I must do it on my own.

I dont think I'll ever be settled now. the best way is to live from day to day. anyway how are you and Dan. I hope happy as usual. why wasnt I like you? Have you herd from Olive?

Nell when you write back dont mention what I wrote if you do put it so I under-stand incase Bill see it.

Oh fuck him say what you want. I'm not starting all that. But not aboat his cloths, I'm glad I gave them away to charity now. Do you no all I've wrote is about myself. How are you doing? I've had some weired things happen in 1 month.

I no I can still pull a fellow, more than what I thought I could. May be I'll find my millionair. 'Dreaming' as usual, but anyway theres a lot in store for me. I know.

Lifes just beginning. My legs do hurt, those stairs! All this for someone you think you love. Anyway love, I'l be closing now.

So God bless love to the children.

Write soon.

Your poor friend Josie

I'll be a different person tomorrow.

Xxxxxxxxx

Write soon Nell

South Africa
1981

Thomas Cook
Cape Town
S.A.

My dear Nell

Thanks a lot for your lovely letter, well my love. I'm please that you and Dan are really getting along with each other. thank you for your lucky charm. A tiny gold fish. I've put it in my locket. And it's always round my neck. Well Nell things are pretty much the same, you would love it, but still very lonley.

They caught Bill fiddling the books and sacked me along with him. I didn't want tell you but the police came for Bill and took him. So Nell Bill is in prison Nell and hes left me living in a garage. I went to see him and they'd put him in a cage. Yes he was in a wire cage. It was horrible.

I wrote back: What's the garage like, Josie?

Well

It's got a concrete floor, quite clean but cold. The toilet is in one corner behind a partition and there is an old Baby Belling in the other. Rusty! No windows except a small one in the toilet and I put my lipstick on in there – the only place with any light. What I hate most is the bit of coconut matting by the bath. It is dark brown and damp and I have to step on it with my bare foot when I get out.

Joey is now living with my mum so I rang him and he wants to come here. as he never got to Australia. He thinks he'll like South Africa. I fill I must try and help him so we have spoke it over and he should be here in the next week. I will fill quite ashamed to bring him to the garage but he will have to understand. Nell I would of come home and sorted it out but I lost my passport and I am waiting for a new one. To top it all my return ticket has run out so I will stay until every think gets settled.

I under-stand Ray has compleatley changed I still wonder how he is and still say a little pray for him. Well it looks like I'm at the bottom again. NO MONEY. I decide I'll leave love & sex out from now on.

I wrote and told Josie that Olive had fallen over and hurt her leg (drunk).

Sorry to here about poor Olive. Please give her my love. I miss her.

Olive had met a vicar who had fallen in love with her. Now her vicar was looking after her. She was living at the vicarage.

I wish my Joey was young again. Still I mustent complain he is still my baby. I wish I never broke our happy family up. What I never had I wouldn't of missed, but fate brought Bill to me. I dont care no more. What will be will be.

God noes whats going to happen I no I cant keep living like this, Bill keeps saying we have to start some where, but I cant seem to bring myself to think that way.

I wrote to Ray and said it was finished. I should of faced him. Bill says no you can't go back. He won't let you go. He'll lock you up.

But I no I should of told him face to face. Ray seems to be gong with anyone & everyone and I no I shouldn't care. May be that's why I cant face him noing he goes with anyone. Who am I to call the kettle black? I cant understand why I care because it has nothink to do with me. I only hope I'm not making another mistake. I do hope Joey understand the way I'm living its such a let down.

South Africa

1981

My dear Nell

Joey has changed his mind. Staying home.

Bill must except me as I am now. I cant give him nothink only my love and heart and most of all my sholder; I'm still willing to give my happy little world up for him? Or am I just trying to be a marter to look up too. do you understand me NELL? I have got to grow up again. Oh I cant explain it not like talking to you. I'm still not sure what I want!. I got so drunk the other night I just danced with every one. Let my hair down it was me senter of actraction, and Nell I loved every minute why I'm like that I no one special I no I showed myself up, still now I'm back to normal. Well my love again I'm still giving you my troubles hurry up and write I so pleased to hear from you. I realy am glad you found Dan.

Well my love take care of your self and keep warm, were a vest. I always think of you.

Good Luck with the play.

My love to you & Dan.

Love always

Josie
Xxxxxx
I'm still fighting the world.
Or is it myself?

Just had a chat with Pearl the young woman who is looking after the house – housekeeper – next door to the garage. We sat on the wall in the sun. She took me indoors and said You can sleep here Mamsel loads of rooms. But the furniture is all covered in white sheets and it gave me the creeps as though someone has died so she took me upstairs and shows me the big 4 poster where she sleeps. 'You can be here with me, plenty room. So tonight you can sleep like a fairy tale princess in a 4 poster bed having sweet dreams.

And so for a week or two, until the owners came home, Josie slept with Pearl and when thinking of Bill in prison she cried. Pearl comforted her. 'Don't cry, Mamsel.'

Pearl, Josie and me

South Africa
1981

My dear Nell

The police couldn't get anything to stick. They had to let Bill go.

Well in one club a man was doing a strip. Well I wanted to join him, can't remember if I did! Anyway I finaly arived back at the garage. I never guessed I'd end up living in a garage. Bill was there. It seem so funny now. anyway next day it all blow over. And I no he loves me. I HOPE and he has his little bit of jealosey, which I'm glad because I used to be terrible over him.

He thinks I'm a flirt. So there no more going out on my own. Nore him, because I wouldn't stop in crying no more. Them days are over. As much as I love him. I don't trust him. He's devious and a liar. Slippery! Never mind. I'm not perfect.

He still turns me on, and I no I do to him now, more than what I did before. I'm glad now I never went with that fellow from the club. He wanted to take me to America. Remember I danced with him half the night? I may of gone to another country but it wouldn't of lasted. Mind you its nice to no I had the chance I would of loved to see Disneyland there but may be I'll get there yet. One day.

I went for a job and haven't heard anything – but some think will come along wont it

Well Nell Bill wants to get married so do I. but we must take things as they come as we must sort ourselfs out as it early days. It feels like we have never been apart is it strange?

Well as for Ray I feel for him terrible and I hope he finds somebody nice who will love him like I do, I found Bill so my love must stay with him for as long as it last. I hope Joey finds what he wants he has a good start. So I've done my duty. So now my life my own, and what ever in my path ahead I must face. I hope I have enough courage.

I often worrie because I seem to have no past, does that seem strange to you?

Its as thou Im talking to you as if you're here. I can see you so plannley. Do me a favour, ring my mum for me send her my love, get her to write.

In a way I'm a prisoner in myself, still not noing what I want. If Bill loves me he must let me face every thing for my own sake, or I'll have no peace.

I no Bill was my knight in shinning armor, and no matter what ever happens I always love him because he gave me some think – 'ME'.

Nell do you no why I love him he make me fill so real, and hes so loving and consideret. makes me a cup of tea in the morning cooks me my supper spends his last two Bob on me. lets me buy nail varnish noing we cant afford it I could go on for ever telling you nice things may be that's what I needed from Ray. he brought me dimonds & minks, and gave me a lovely home but I needed the small things and lots of love and affection. Ray's house was full of beautiful antique furniture and it was like a museum, He'd nicked it all of course. And he shouted at me if I overdid his steak. He was angry all the time.

I need loving so much, I've give all my love to ever body else, and I no deep down thats all I wanted kindness. but the world will never go round by love and kindness its too hard. So enjoy the small things in life there more precious than people think.

There still many people that are being hurt through me, and it is cruel, and even to Joey I brought him in to the world then I must help him on the right path, not run away from him, it doesnt matter what he thinks of me, of course I care but he still needs a mother to run too. this has always been my down fall, my week ness or am I just trying to hang on to him.

Do you no Nell I sat down the beach yesterday on my own. God it was parridise, But no one to talk to, no gossip; its alright getting lovely & Brown but no one to see it. I want the simple life like a beach comer, no worrie no dressing up. Then may be I'll find what I really want, out of life.

It was so hot, did I tell you? I've learnt to swim. Well almost. At least paddle in up to my waist. Well love theres no more to tell you today so I'll close. God bless love. I'm keeping my fingers crossed for Steaming.

    Josie

I'm glad you and Dan made beauty love, make it stay like it love. Because thats what makes every day a bit more lovely. I tell you what Nell I do feel a different person. My body feels alive. Darling I close now as I am just popping out. Xxx

Josie and I continued to miss Olive.

I remembered our visiting her.

Visiting Olive

I think we should go to Reading and see Olive she isn't well, said Josie. She'd had another fall and more or less given up on Old Compton Street.

Reading was where Olive had been living when she wasn't working. Now her vicar had taken her in permanently. We went on the train. Olive met us. She didn't look well but she wanted us to meet her friend.

The vicar lived in a great big red-brick house next to the church. He made us welcome. He told us he had fallen in love with Olive.

Olive sat on a chair smiling her mysterious smile. She wanted a drink and the vicar fetched a bottle of sherry and four glasses and some biscuits. We drank to Olive's health. And then to the vicar's health. He topped up our glasses and Olive started to sing a hymn she remembered from Sunday school.

What a friend we have in Jesus.

Josie joined in. And so did the vicar.

What a privilege to carry everything to God in prayer.

The vicar sang in a strong baritone. Olive in a reedy falsetto. And Josie in a sweet lyrical soprano.

I did my best!

Soon in glory bright unclouded there
Will be no need for prayer
Rapture, praise and endless worship
Will be our sweet portion there.

The vicar took out a handkerchief and wiped his brow.

I think this calls for another drink!

And having finished the sherry, Olive sipping with pleasure and licking her lips, the vicar broke into song again.

Oh have we trials and temptations?
Is there trouble anywhere?
We should never be discouraged
Take it to the Lord in prayer.

And the vicar, after striking a few notes on the harmonium, took Olive gently on his knee and rocked her for the final verse.

Can we find a friend so faithful
Who will all our sorrows share
In his arms he'll take and shield thee?
Take it to the Lord in prayer.

I think we'd better go, Josie!

Time to catch our train.

We said goodbye to the vicar and he whispered in my ear, 'I love her, and I'll never let her go.'

And Olive took us to the door and as she said goodbye a secret smile lit up her delicate face.

And so we left them and hurried hand in hand to get the bus to the station and home.

Goodbye, Vicar.

Goodbye, Olive.

Mucking about: Josie, Olive and me

South Africa
1981

My dear Nell,

Well love by now you must of resived my letter. So write back. I'm waiting.

I'm still plodding along but so terrible lonley inside, I try and explain how I feel to Bill he doesn't understand. He has a new job selling built-in wardrobes so we've got a flat now. Not bad. Better than the garage. When he gets angry all hes says is what do I want out of life no one will ever satisfie me as if I'm a freak.

Do you no Nell even the other day I was jealose not of Bill, But to think he had lunch at this lovely place although it was business but to me its pleaser as well, I no I'm gready for lovely things and lovely places because that's when I feel alive.

I got drunk again on purpose the night he came home. Why I don't know. because I haven't for 6 weeks. I hated life again am I such a selfish person? I hated him having a good time without me. Am I becoming like a hateful bitch? Some time I want to be hatefull, because I gave every think up so Bill must put all his time into me, I no it doesnt work like that Nell. but I feel a nobody and I hate it. You no what I mean? I dont feel the ego that I had before. the fight inside me, I feel like an every day person, remmber when I used to say I must never become an surburn house wife, well thats how I feel. may be that what I am, realy.

But what the fuck do I want to be? I no I'm the same as everyone eles, no better no worse, and every time Bill says grow up, I hate him. Not HATE REALY but I dont want to grow up!

I never realy looked after myself realy, I grew up to quik,and when I felt a reck and deprest like I am now you gave me a lift. My mum would say you can pick and shoes who you want.

Ray would by me a new present to make me happy, its as thou I have no-one to cheer me up no more. And although Bill gives me what he can its not enough. I wouldnt tell him. I couldn't hurt his feelings.

Its ok for Bill this is his country, he can bump into a friend or even his brother, Me I have no one, I've made friends Nell but I seem to of closed up inside me, sometimes I go to work cleaning in a bar and make out I'm so happy and nice to every one. What is happning to me?

May be its because I had to much, to quick, Im used to the best or nearly the best. I wish I never thought big, but I have tried not thinking like that realy I have. I feel like I'm missing somethink in my life. 'YET I'M not' everydays the same, we wash eat go to work, sleep, have 'happy days' and 'sad days' were all the same, I was thinking of going to see a sicartrise I think I told you but will he be able to help me? Or must I help myself? As I say it feels like I never had no past, its a strange feel. Nell, I dont want to drink, but I drink for the sake of it.

Do you no I hate the thought of Bill having more sex than me, so childish I never been like this, and I think its because I'm alone, its not as thou I can pop round the corner and have a chat with you, I no I drive and meet people and talk to them, but I'm still alone. So Fucking alone. Its as thou my adventures have come to an end I must settle down

Bill thinks I always want to be in the lime light is that so bad?

When I finish my cleaning work I come home, to what. 4 walls wait for Bill to come home maybe be 5.30 may 6-0 who noes what time Im here between 4-o/4.30 oh fuck. I'm borde, I dont no if I can keep it up, I wish somethink nice would happen.

May be I'm still looking. I just dont no now. Well it will all work out I'm shore, I try not to think of the past Nell but when I sit alone I do and Bill is the past realy, yet I cant do with out him. he seem to feed me. I no now we iratate each other.

On my side is because I wont grow up and face life. I said he must find a woman who like sitting at home, I wasnt born that way and now its Because I always been spoilt and so on. May be its true, he said I must be the good Josie, she cant do nothink wronge.

90

I could go on and on. So now I'm going to try it his way come home cooke the dinner etc I'll just die then Nell. Anyway if I dont like it I'll get out. I met Bill 1st Wife Sunday Margret. I wasnt bitchey but humiliated. I felt rather sorry, she about 46, been a nice looking woman but lives alone now with her two cats. I'll die if I become like her she has no mum or dad no family. I looked at her & him its not me Nell.

Well love he'll be in soon so I have to close. My love to Dan and kids. Look after yourself.

Hope Steaming goes good!

Wish me luck to-morrow for New job in a hotel.

See You Nell. God Bless love

From Josie xxxxx

Xxxx

What shall I do? fancy asking you. Well I have to get myself out. I got myself into it.

But I pressing on regardless, I start my job Monday. Hotel receptionist. I think I've been here before so fingers cross for me, Oh love I'm always telling you my problem art I? 'YES Josie'

So Nell hurry up and write it seems ages since I hered from you.

So until I here from you. Keep happy, both of you.

My love to the kids, and your Mum and Dan.

See you soon.

All my love always

Love Josie xxxxx

This letter kept you busy for 5 minutes, I want a long one from you.

And I wrote one. I told her how Dan had moved into my house and I couldn't stand it! Either of us.

He was coming down from Islington on his motorbike every evening and I said, 'I can't stand this!' Move in!

So he did and he put all his clothes in my cupboard and there wasn't room for my clothes but he's still here! I make it sound horrible but really it is great (and he's a wonderful cook!). But driving each other nuts! We share the bath. I love that. Taking all the kids away in the summer – wild camping in the camper van.

I had thought of becoming an ambulance driver. It might be more adventurous than being a writer but you had to do nights and I'm a very slow driver. Another thing: I don't like driving in the dark.

And I was still writing.

(Being a writer is so lonely.)

South Africa
1981

Hallow Nell

Well my love your letter was so lovely. Hang on to Dan and don't be selfish. I know what you are like with hangers. Greedy!

Nell your never lose my friendship. Because you mean so much in my life. Nell. Well so you want to be an Ablance driver. You can do it! It is a new chalange for you. Oh Nell I love you so much as my best friend, Nell I no you get a kick out of life like me, I live – you have beatiful fanterys and you dont see the bad side, – and I sometimes I don't like it. So stay as you, and remmber every think will always be beatiful then.

Now Nell I envy you walking down North End Rd even if its cold and rainy. How are you and Dan I hope well and happy and having laugh.

Well Nell Bill had a slite heart Atack. Real shame. He is only 50. Oh it has worry me but he much better now.

Well I've been offered a proper job now tell you more when I start it. I wish it had been in London but I wouldn't have the chance there.

Nell I hope I start a carrier here I do so much want some think in life, somethink for myself to fight for. Its not much to ask for is it. I always said I would love to be you to be somebody but as you said, I am somebody not fammose but a real person. But that sounds Big Headed.

As I sayd my return ticket run out so I have GOT to make it. I had my chance to turn back if I wanted to. I never so I must make the most of it and most of all make it. I can't afford the flight home.

Tell Dan to look after you and Nell when he bys those nice little presents no matter whos there get up and kiss him and say thanks, dont wait till your on your own its not the same. Now I'm lecturning you.

I had a nice letter from my mum, well it was a bit sad I was so chocked but I do love her so much I never relise. I miss her nagging me and telling me about her boyfriend Arthur. God I never realised how lucky I am. I MEAN THAT. Well Nell dont forget to write as much as you can. Because I love hearing from you. Hows all the family? hope all well, Nell, well thats about it love so until I here from you.

Best of luck with the Abulance driver job.

Love always

Josiexxxxxx

I never became an ambulance driver. I didn't pass the test. I drive too slowly.

The Cruise

I remember our trip down the Nile and how we had quarrelled when she took all the hangers.

'You've taken more than half the hangers.'

'Well, I've got more clothes than you.'

And a serious quarrel.

'I tell you how nice you look and you never tell me I'm looking nice.'

'Let me get my fags and sit down then I can think.'

'Well, you'd better think that I look nice.'

Later we sat on wooden deckchairs side by side. We each had a cocktail and sipped as we glided gently up the Nile.

Two small boys were fishing among the reeds. The last of the sunshine was dappling our feet.

Josie: I do miss you.

Nell: And I miss you.

Josie: We've had some lovely times.

Nell: Yes, really really lovely times.

South Africa
1981

My dear Nell

How are you love? Well Nell I've had a long think about me and Bill, and I dont no what to do I'm going to give it a few more weeks then I will no then. Yes he got me a new job doing as Marketin Exeketiv. at the wardrobe place. Fuck noes what that means. So here I am washed and dressed in a big car and I don't know where I am going.

Iff this job was in London it would be great. I always wanted to be somebody but I no it can never be over there.

Nell my life seems so hard to me now. I'm not happy now but very lonley. I cant settle with Bill he's changed. I'm not deprest, I relize Ive made a miss take so I must right it myself. I had another fight with Bill, but it was bad this time hes become an animal or may be its me. I dont love him I thought I did, but I wont let it get me down. Your letter brought me to my senceses.

I wrote: I am so far away and you in another country. Josie, don't you think you should pack up and come home?

I have got to stand on my own feet and I will. I've got to! Now to you. How are you love? and Dan and the kids are you more happier now and not so lost? Your letter up set me a little bit, because I never relised how I depended on you, funny realy.

I'm going to dinner with this new fellow on Thursday and I'm going. I dont care if Bill find out, I'm going to make the most of it while Im here. Well love try and under-stand I love you as a good friend, and one day were look back on all this and say Fuck me it was all worth it. Oh Im lucky realy to of lived it, because you cant buy expenrece, you have to live it as you say you must have the good times with the bad but I dont like the bad. Well my love I'll close now. So write soon as your letter keep me alive.

How is Steaming going?

God bless Nell love to Dan

Love Josie

Xxxxx

Xxxx

(I'LL MAKE IT YET WITH ALL MY MISTAKES)

Your old friend Josie xxxxxxxx

For better or worse

P.S. Remember that Winter afternoon wanting luxury and adventure we went to the Floation Tank on Clapham Common?

And I remembered and wrote about it in *My Silver Shoes* in 1996.

Josie takes off her clothes and folds them neatly and puts them on the seat of the chair. I hang mine over the back. It isn't a posh place. In fact we were told we should have brought our own towels. The young man with the ponytail finds us a couple of small ones with frayed ends.

'Don't let go of my hand.'

'I won't. Just shut your eyes and relax.'

Floating side by side in the dark warm water. Holding her little bird-like hand as if I was holding just the thin bones, no flesh.

'My back is going to break in two,' said Josie. 'Don't turn out the light. I can't breathe.'

'Let go, let go, darling.'

'Ahh, I'm floating.'

The tips of her breasts, her nipples, protruded from the dark water.

Her knees, the bones of her hips, all bones like the small bunch of bones in my hand. I move my fingers between her fingers.

She sighs.

'Turn out the light.'

I reach up and turn out the small dim light. Now we are in pitch black floating, the salty water the same temperature as the air, as our blood.

'Am I still here?'

'Yes, feel my hand.'

'I thought I might be dead.'

'You're alive.'

'Yes, I'm alive. I can hear my heart beating.'

'Lie quiet.'

'Ahh. I'm so still.'

I hold the small hand while I listen to her breathing change and she sleeps. I don't want to sleep but to guard her sleep, her fragile hand in mine, and listen to her breathing. My princess sleeps and I lie beside her in the dark water very wide awake in the pitch silence.

Josie and me in the 1970s on Clapham Common

South Africa
1981

My dear Nell

Well love sorry for not writing sooner but realy Nell this Marketin Execative job realy keeps me going it's a good job, as I say, I wish I had it in London. well anyway I've been permoted now as an area manager . Yes! I'm coming up in the world,

Nell I'm trying to save so I can afford to come home, but I do feel a little insecure but I will face that when it come to it. Hard to save as things are very dear here.

How you and Dan? I hope well. DAN KEEP HER UNDER CONTROLL.

Nell I'm not in love with Bill, but I like being with him, and he can do a lot for me besides trouble. The job was due to him so one thing I must thank him fo.

He seems to have aged, got very serose and me, well I've gone wild Well my sex life isn't so good now funny how things change. 'Sham realy' I met a nice fellow the other day. He said my eyes talk. Fuck me he was handsum but married so best left alone

'NEWS FLASH!'. I have a company car now. Volse Wagon nice and new I have a casset in it. Oh Nell there a

record or casset you must get 'DON'T LEAVE ME THIS WAY' Oh you and Dan will love it. FOR ME get it love its got lovely meaning and words.

I no now I'll never settle here ll but Nell the job is somethink I always wanted so may be I'll be lucky? Now I would rather have a nice carreyer (although I cant spell)? I do it on my own merits I don't feel degraded here having no equcation. Because they dont no I come from England I can tell many lies and no one noes.

How have you been love? I do miss you. Well my darling I'll be closing now write soon. My love to Dan as always tell him to give you a big kiss and be happy always. Write soon love because I need your letters and remmber live your life, for good days and Bad days.

God Bless. Things will get better.

Love Josiexxxx

Meantime Dan was struggling with his job. He had huge responsibilities for government computer programs and they would keep changing the brief and he was ordered by someone who knew nothing about computers to do impossible tasks. I struggled to be supportive. I was a staunch feminist and didn't want to get swallowed up in my partner's problems, however much I loved him. Looking back I know I didn't do enough.

Nell and Josie on the phone:

Nell: Can we ever get it right?

Josie: We can be loving and tell them we love them but it's never enough. I always want more – more money, better job. I've been lucky, but I want more.

Nell: Me too. Like my mum says: More fun!

South Africa
1981

My dear Nell

Well love it was lovely talking to you and to no you are happy again and your still in love and having lovely peace-full moments.

Well Nell aboat the phone bill all I have is £50 which I am sending a cheque for. I no its not the full amount but how on earth it came to 70 pounds I'll never no. Was that for having it instaled to? I would rather Joey have only incoming calls from now on could you mention it to him. he'll take notice of you.

Nell I no how humanating it is when you go for an interview and they keep you waiting around and they don't say yes or no it horrible. And thats why Joey has given up. Unless you've experinsed it yourself you cant feel the demoralise feeling. If a person applies for a job they must be told yes or no if they have been excepted. the worst thing of all is when they have already imployed some one and they haven't taken the advert out or even got intouch with the employment agency, Oh Nell its a horrible feeling not to of been given the chance, noing you coperbale of doing it. look at me I cant spell but I try.

You should see me trying to spell Africkans, I cant even spell English right.

Oh remmber the pain in my neck and head & throat. Well I think I found out why I went to a dentis here hes a specialist I cant think what hes called anyway its to do with that crown tooth I had. I had a bad habit of grinding my teeth which has caused the tention in some nerve. Anyway he gave me some pills which I have to take before I go to sleep to stop the tention. I go back again Wednesday so I'll tell you more than. Im going to make shore I have the best treatment while I can. I do hope it helps. To think I went to hospital doctor ostrepath, I hope it does cure it, I would feel much better in myself so keep your finger cross.

Did Joan tell you I'm not drinking too much now. I dont enjoy it. Fuck noes what I enjoy now.

We have a new colour lady now. She nice she said she goes to church Sunday. I said say a pray for me. Oh yes Madam I will. She said she happy she works for me everybody talks about the little english Madam Me!

Well its Tuesday to-day I dont feel so fed up but I cant make myself out I just don't no what I want.

Bill said a lot of home truths aboat me and its made me think, what type of person am I? I can feel myself changing he said all I say I want to live go dancing buy lovely cloths. I dont or wont stand up to my responcerbilitys. I think I have become like that. I always looked at Bill as someone to take that burden away from me. but hes becoming stale or may be its me.

I no he has a very good new job but it's all he can talk about. (He has to take care of all the cigarette machines in the clubs – 3 people under him. Don't ask me what he does! I don't no. I hope he noes.)

I no its for both of us he does it but I feel left out although I have a lovely job its not enough I must feel that light inside me. its as thow I'm dead inside, he give's me every think he can. but not himself. Why am I so greedy for life happness love why are they so hard to find?

Love your friend

Josie

Leaving Bill and South Africa
1981

Josie told me what happened

One morning I woke up.

Bill had gone to work.

It was building up for a month. I knew I couldn't take it no more.

He got pulled up for handling uncut diamonds again. Never told me but I know he was going to be done for stolen jewellery as well.

They were after him.

And I woke up sweating.

The lies!

But I don't know what happened; it just came over me and I rang Ray and he paid the fare and I left everything behind and got a taxi to the airport.

When I got home what happened was I went back with Ray – after all, he paid the fare.

He bought me all new clothes but Ray wasn't really good to me. He didn't let me forget he'd paid my fare. He bossed me around. Shouted at me. Called me a whore!

When they hurt you you close down.

Sex doesn't work.

So I left him. And I took the new clothes.

And I went back to Sissy, my mum. It was over for me and Ray. And over for me and Bill.

Josie went back to live with Sissy. She got a job in the local pub. Soon after, Bill had a serious heart attack and died.

Josie cried when she heard. She told me how.

I was standing at the bus stop on my way to work. Ray drew up in his Mercedes and wound down the window.

He's dead! Your fancy man is dead. Heart attack!

And he drove off.

It was raining and people were looking and I turned away and I cried.

Nell

1981

I was having a really difficult time trying to get *Steaming* on. But no one wanted it: 'How could you have a pool and a lot of naked women on stage?'

I always forget that an important part of a writer's life is to persuade the publisher or a producer to read your work – let alone like it and back it.

It is painful because you are asking for something that often gets refused. And you have to cope. Like Josie being turned down for a job.

In desperation I went to the stage door of the Duke of York's Theatre and left a copy of *Steaming* for Roger Smith who was directing the play there called *Duet for One* by Tom Kempinski, which I thought was wonderful. I knew Roger but hadn't seen him for years. Two days later he rang me and said, 'Yes, I will direct *Steaming*. I like it.'

So Christopher Malcolm and Roger and Eddie Kulukundis got together with Philip Hedley who ran the Theatre Royal, Stratford East and it happened. *Steaming* opened at the Theatre Royal, Stratford East with Georgina Hale playing Josie in July 1981. Josie and Dan were beside me for the first night.

And I shall never forget Georgina Hale as Josie, jumping on a chair, half-naked, to deliver an impassioned speech furiously demanding the baths should stay open for ordinary people.

After the show we 'went round'. There is something very glamorous about 'going round', to go down the narrow stone passages and up little staircases. Then into the dressing room – an Aladdin's cave of delight, cards and flowers like talismans to success all around the room. A couch across one wall so she could rest before the stage manager knocked for the half and fear might strike. But after the show all was glorious. We opened the champagne and toasted the actors. Then for a moment Josie was the centre of attention, she too was toasted. And theatre is the bravest of the arts.

Acting is an amazing act of courage. There is nothing quite like it.

Josie in Spain
1981

After the brief time with Ray, and living with with Sissy, her mother, in Roehampton Hill, one day Josie woke up bored and broke. So she borrowed some money and headed for the Costa Brava and a job running a beach bar.

Torreblanca

Dear Nell

Well love time you get this letter you be home from Greese and I hope you enjoyed it not to much work. I no its as lovely as Spain. I also hope thoss Blue days have gone and its done you good. <u>thank you</u> Nell for the money it was a lovely surprise. The phone hasent been put on but its so Manyana here!

Still wondering what am I to do? So Im going to carry on. I hope you come out to visit soon.

Oh yes I got the gas fire. So much hassell as the certificate is – another £40 but its new and safe so I'm ok. Got that Big Mirror take up all the wall over the settie your love it (second Hand) White 6ft long found it in the paper drove the man mad. So thats enough of me.

I no you must feel lonley some times. We cant just ring each other and have a long chat. But love if you ever realy feel down I'll pop over. I think I'll come back in Oct. for a week, although I'm frighten too. why? I dont no.

Send my love to Dan. When things are nice over here I think I'm only here on holiday but I do get down days Nell. I think of Joey but he is going his separate way. I feel like I've always been a loaner. I think Nell my fire went out for a long time I was so lost inside of me not noing which way to go, and I was letting life pass me by just like the wind. I am going to try hard to settle for as long as I can. I cant face coming home yet. I still worry but not as much as I did. At the moment I feel I've been here for ever in my little world. I do hope Ivy leg is better (poor little cow) its must have been so painfull for her and not forgetting May. (Give them a bisket from me).

My dogs. Ivy, my Jack Russell, broke her leg.

I feel like being on my own. It doesnt worry me at the moment I've been here nearly 2 month on the 21st. Well love take care of yourself Keep your chin up, think of our lovely time we had in Parades El-Costillo our carsal. And you taught me to swim at last! Without the Rubber Ring!

Oh yes I went to Los Bolishes Town Hall for Spanish Lesson its moved to Fenjerolo Town Hall another place to find can never rember the names of the Street but remmber how to get there.

Oh yes I am working in the beach bar (God it is hard work in this heat) 4 afternoons a week. Still I enjoyed it, chatting away to every one oh it was funny they thought I owned it. I told them I'm only the 'washer up'. But maybe one day. I like Spain.

Well love that's aboat it no more news I will ring you next week. Remember come out again soon!

Lots of love always and to Ivy poor little cow.

Josie xxx

Alhambra Palace Hotel

P.S. JOSIE: I met a very nice man called Tony. He wants to take me out.

And this was the start of a new romance with Tony, an older man.

He wants to take me out to The Alhambra Palace hotel.

Tony took Josie to the Alhambra Palace Hotel. And they stayed the night.

Josie: *This must be the most beautiful view in the world. What are those mountains called?*
Tony: *Those are the Sierra Nevada.*
Josie: *Come here quickly! The sun is getting up and the mountains are all bright pink!*

Tony and Josie

Tony was running away from something, but I never found out what. A lot of Brits go to Spain to get away from their lives in England.

Now Josie was with him we could talk on the telephone.

But not that often – or Tony grumbled.

Josie: *I've given up the beach bar. Tony says he'll give 'pocket money'!*

My dear nell

I'm beginning to wonder how much money Tony has. Maybe he fucked up his busniss and his wife chucked him out. Perhaps one day he'll tell me. But he definitely isn't a Big Spender.

Meanwhile, I told him, 'I see you as my Prince Charming. At long last you have come. I see you as a millionaire who needs cheering up.'

I think I worried him!

That's every woman's dream and I thought it had happened to me. I saw him as my Saviour. My way out. My ticket to Fairyland where everything is fresh and clean. A terrace with plants. My sun lounger with its yellow umbrella.

Meanwhile back at the Theatre Royal, Stratford East, Georgina Hale as Josie is lying naked on the marble side of the pool.

Josie: *'I'd like to just lie here and have people pay to come look at me.'*

A man's voice shouting from the balcony: 'I have paid and I am looking.'

And the good news is *Steaming* was going to transfer to the West End.

Eddie Kulukundis took me to look at theatres.

And we chose the Comedy Theatre, now called the Harold Pinter.

In a curious way, although I was thrilled, really, really thrilled, it felt unreal as though it was happening to someone else a long way away.

Steaming opened on 20 August 1981 at the Comedy Theatre. Dan and Josie were with me. That winter snow fell and came through the back of the stage and the actors were naked and cold.

Dan was a backer and he was pleased because he made some money!

And the farmers arrived from Smithfield Market and filled the theatre every night and one night they made so much noise whistling that Georgina (our Josie) stepped to the front of the stage and said to the audience, 'Unless you shut up we won't carry on!' There was immediate silence and the play went on.

Olive

Olive was drinking too much. She was still spending a lot of time at the vicarage but she was drinking not praying and we were worried.

Being an alcoholic can make you suicidal. And Olive was very depressed. In spite of her loving vicar.

Reading

Dear Nell

Just a few lines to let you know that I thought it best if I sent the check on too you by Post, I am too depressed at the moment to do anything, but don't worry I will phone you as soon as I feel a bit better, I have wrote a letter to Josie thanking her for her card.

Nell love, between me and you I'm not getting any better really, I just seem to be getting worse, at this moment as I'm writing this letter, I'm much better dead than alive, I don't seem to be any good to any one even myself and my Mum and Dad. I don't see why they should suffer anymore than they have, down to me.

Lots of Love

From your
Friend Olive
Xxxxxx
Xxxxxx

P.S. give my love to the children. I would love to see you and Josie again. I am still living with my vicar but he worried about me and we are both addicted to sherry.

My dearest Olive

Your letter made me sad. Last time we met we had such fun.

You sang hymns with the vicar, not always in tune, but a beautiful voice and it comes flooding back.

Hang in there, Olive and we will go to Antigua and sit on the beach and drink Pina Coladas and be carefree.

Do you remember that swing in the playground? (Just a memory to make you smile!)

I sat on it and you pushed and then you pushed me too high and I slipped off the seat and fell on my head with my legs in the air. I saw stars!

Thinking of you with love.

Nell

P.S. You looked beautiful in the Carnival dress. Thanks for the photo. I will come soon.

Spain
1981

Tuesday

Dearest Nell

*I'm back here with Tony. It was a lovely visit to London.
My Mum cried when I left. And I've told Tony all about
STEAMING and how lovely Georgina looked.*

*Sorry aboat my writing but Ive broken my nail and its
quite painfull. Yes I'll be back by March so were both go
and see Steaming with Carol White and I hope she plays
Josie as good as she played Joy but thinking back its better
to be an actress to play the part but to live it is much
harder as you know.*

Carol had played Joy, based on Josie, in the film of
my novel *Poor Cow*.

*Staying here I've had a lot of hours to think of myself, and
I feel quite a different person. You sertaley dont get nothing
for nothing. Tony has showed me a different way of life.*

*I only wished he was a younger man. but if he was I
dont surpose I'd be here, so I must enjoy every moment of*

my stay. He's quite a loverble person, he said that I'm a perfect woman! and he doesnt want to loose me he thinks I'm so warm and loving and wants to spend the rest of his life with me. I felt very sad last night and very tearful and he just comforted me I cant explain the feeling I had. but he was there and we talked for a couple of hours about our lives.

He asked me to come out here to live permentley, I dont know what to do. Yes its pardise at the moment. But noing me I'd get fed up.

He hit the nail on the head about me. He said I dont know what I do want, but he would like to help me try and find myself. I told him a bit aboat my life but not to much. Still I wont go into that now.

Nell I'm glad 'Steaming' doing well and Lord Snowden takin your photo 'NEWS FLASH' still it's a lovely honor, keep one for me. I proud of you and gelose. How's Dan and the boys? Send them my love.

Time going quite quick here. Well my love I'll write again soon but I want to post this letter today. So look after yourself. Keep warm write soon.

Love Josie xxxx

P.S.
Weather not to bad here. Poor you in the cold.

Steaming at the Comedy Theatre

Steaming transfers to the Comedy Theatre and Josie and Dan and I sit together in a box on the first night.

After the show we went round. And it is extraordinary to see the actors assume their real-life personas.

And they hugged Josie and Georgie said her character was wonderful and it was an honour to play her.

And later, after lots of hugging and kissing backstage, we went to Joe Allen's where Josie led a conga in and out of the tables and we danced till morning.

What a strange time in my life.

After a few weeks Georgina Hale left to go on to other things and Carol White took over.

They were so different.

Georgie all feisty and wonderfully alive.

Carol slow and gorgeous.

Josie and I would often go backstage after the show and when there was no champagne someone would make a cup of tea.

Meanwhile a bit of scenery had dislodged itself from the

roof and fallen and hit Brenda Blethyn. Big to-do. We all thought the show would have to close. All the cast in tears. I was in tears, too.

But after a three-day recovery break – they were all back at work.

Business as usual. Brave Brenda.

Carol White and me on the set of Poor Cow

Spain
1982

Los Boliches

Malaga

My dear nell

*Well my love I bet your wondering why I havent wrote?
This is the first day I've felt OK. I havent felt to good.
Things are much the same here. very quiet but that does
me good. Quitens me down. How Dan & boys I hope well?*

*Well Nell I had some more lovely Red Roses today never
had it so good. Oh yes. Tony thought you were delightful to
speak to him on the phone.*

*How is Carol getting on? I want to see her again! Now
she has taken over from Georgie.*

*Do you remember when we took Carol on Joan's river
boat up the Thames? And Joan made us those Vodka
coktals? And Carol didn't know what hit her.*

She wanted to see you, Josie, so she could act you.

*Give all my love to all the girls in the play. Tony is realy
sweet, but your never belive what happen yesterday I got*

ready to go out last night and then he felt to tired. So I had a few drinks and went to bed. So at least I can control myself at present.

So I think I can make a Lady for a month (I hope).

We had a party in Tony's apartment. Invited the Old Brits from the bar – terribly posh. By the end I had them all singing 'I've got a lovely bunch of coconuts'!

Now dont forget to write will you and tell me all the new's. I had a nice letter from my mum today. Oh I was so pleased, although I'm not feeling home sick yet. I cant say much at the moment as Tony writing to his sister across the table – but will write soon and tell you more. I havent had much time to write down whats happening as Tony always behind me, anyway I'll close now my love, take care write soon. Be lucky.

Look after yourself

Love from Josie

Xxxxx

Steaming on Broadway
1982

In December 1982 *Steaming* opened on Broadway and Josie and I flew to New York, first class. And Dan joined us.

We all stayed at the Algonquin and none of us could sleep so we talked all night and the next day was the first night of *Steaming* at the Brooks Atkinson on Broadway.

Josie and I had our hair done on Fifth Avenue and when we came to pay the bill we didn't have enough money and the salon insisted someone accompany us to the bank – 'But she's got a play on Broadway,' said Josie.

'Oh yeah!' said the hairdresser. We were still wearing our gowns and we walked down Madison Avenue in our pink gowns all the way to the bank.

And after the show there was a party at Sardi's and the producer paged Josie (she loved it). Then the reviews started to come in and they were bad, really BAD. (But Judith Ivey won a Tony Award for playing Josie.) I saw the video of her (Judith) going to receive her prize in front of an audience of hundreds.

The next day Josie, Dan and I flew home.

The Broadway run closed on 5 February 1983 after sixty-five performances.

Spain and Tony
1982

Hotel Alhambra Palace

Alhambra Palace, S.A.

H****

Granada (España)

Saved the writing paper from when we stayed here!

My dear Nell

Well love how are you? I heard you won another award.
An Olivier award?

Very pleased for you. I seem to be missing all these
lovely nights out, still never mind, I have only resived one
letter from you. 'Whys that?' I hope you resived mine and
the card? I thought this note paper looks good, it was in
our room so being you specil I had to write to you on it.

Well 3 weeks have nearly gone so time you resive this
letter I will be home. back to <u>Earth</u>, which I'm not looking
forward to. We have been to lots of places and I've enjoyed
it very much, I sent a card to Olive, oh yes.

Joan went to see the play loved it. She said you give her
the tickets. Give my love to Dan and the boys.

Oh love I went to a cemetery yesterday. Oh it was sad, they put you in a hole and cement it up. It was an America fellow. He was a Vitnam War herow, poor sod. He had pots of money yet buried out here you thought they would of flown him home, but will tell you more when I see you.

I've met lots of new people one lady in pertickler, she wants me to stay on and we will drive back to England later but Tony insists I go by plane because its dangers. (Jealouse realy) if he had his way I'll be in a big buble so no one could breath on me but he's quite sweet. I've got drunk a few times but he still loves me, he thinks I've had such a rough deal in life, but as I've explained to him my life up to now hasent been too bad.

He wants to make a Will out here as he hasent done up to now, but that could be all talk. You no I always wanted some one to plonk it in my hand but being here has made me think twice. You may not belive it love but I feel quite a diffrent person. I cant explain it Nell much slower in my thinking. I dont know if it's a good thing or bad. May be it's a turning point how I entend to go on in life.

Well my love theres no more to tell you, only keep well and we will have a nice day out together when I return home. I've been very spoilt out here, and will miss it terribly back in Putney. He wants me to live out here for good, so I'll have to think realy hard, wont I but I think I mentioned that in my last letter. At least I've had the offer, of some one giving me something instead of the other way round. Men I found up to now want every thing from me. I do wish Tony was 20 year's younger. Then my dreams would of all come true. it makes me a bit sad, I imajin so many things what it would have been like. A bit like the scene in the play. You know – the one where she lies naked by the pool and has all those fantasies? But much better and different. Remind me to tell you the fantersey about being in the 40s with Tony Oh your love it.

Its now time I washed and dressed for dinner were going to 'Grandpa' tonight a lovely restrunt, Oh and I have to wear my red Rose on my Black suit (you would think I was going to a wedding) but I wear it for him, he tell's me I'm lovely every five minutes and my blue eyes shine like the sea, I dont no how he thinks of all the things he says. Well my love the paper's running out and I must dash now and get ready.

My love always

Josie xxx

'The princess from the moon'

(THAT'S Tony) I said its like a story)

And I told him my fantersy – he is all dressed up in a kernals uniform with his medals on his chest and his silver hair and silver mustash all btifully combed.

And I'm in a blood red and silver lamé dress and I have these blood red shoes. Silk they are with very high heels and I hold your arm and we walk down this beautiful stercase and our song is playing . . . when the night has come. And the world is still. And everyone is watching.

But I had to say goodbye. I felt really sad. He loved me.

And so Josie left Tony.

Leaving Tony
1982

As Josie Told Me

That was sad when I left him. I always felt guilty.

What happened was: 'I'm going down to the Tall Man (our bar) to make a phone call to Sissy.'

He had had his home phone cut off – he thought it was too expensive – I was making too many calls to my mum.

Then he wouldn't have a television. He said television was too expensive.

'We'll listen to Gib on the radio for the news.'

I was going out of a daytime. I wasn't working. I was living a nice life.

But when someone 'looks after you' you have to do what they want. And I've always done what I wanted.

I got bored.

You have to answer to them.

He was an older gentleman.

He'd ask me where I'd been. If I went to the bar he'd time me.

But I loved him. I'd always wanted a man who adored me but when I got it – it was too much.

I had to leave. I felt really sorry – he loved me.

Tony loved me. But he was so jealous I had to go. He'd roar if I came back late. Roar like a lion and I didn't like it.

I heard afterwards it had broken his heart – me leaving.

They found him dead with a long white beard. I was really sorry. I cried. Couldn't stop crying when I heard.

But I had to go.

Then in 1984 Joseph Losey made a film of Steaming.

Patricia, Joe's wife, wrote the screenplay.

I introduced Josie to them and she became their housekeeper.

As Josie Told Me

Patricia was in Paris and Mr Losey, I always called him Mr Losey, although he told me to call him Joe, said he was hungry.

I'm hungry, Josie.

I cooked eggs, bacon, sausages, tomatoes and beans. He ate it all. He couldn't believe it. Then he said, 'Go round the corner and get a bottle of Polonez vodka and we'll have a drink.'

And I ran round the corner – he had to write the name down for me on a piece of paper so I got the right one – and I came back with the special vodka and he said, 'You have one too.'

We sat on the steps outside the house on Royal Avenue, it was a lovely summer and we talked about life and all the interesting things we'd done.

I was studying reflexology at the time so I did his feet.

He loved it.

One day when Patricia was in Paris and we had been drinking vodka on the front step I said, 'Oh fuck, I'm drunk. I'd better not drive home.'

He was pissed too.

'Leave your car here,' he said.

And he called a taxi. And he paid the driver and sent me home. He was good to me and so was Patricia. Very kind to me.

They treated me like a friend.

I felt very sad when he died. He got very ill and died quickly. Patricia was broken-hearted.

Diana Dors, who was in Joe's *Steaming*, died too. She was a beautiful woman.

It was a very sad summer.

Joe died in June 1984 and Diana Dors in May 1984.

They had hardly finished filming.

After Joe died Patricia went to live in Paris.

Josie in the 1990s. Still magnificent

Late that summer Josie was back working on 'the boats' with Joan and living with Sissy.

Up and down the bloody Thames behind the bar. With Joan. Bloody hard work!

And sometimes I got pissed. You get pissed twice as fast on water. Did you know that, Nell?

Meanwhile I started to think about *My Silver Shoes*, the third book I wrote about Josie – calling her Joy – and Sissy. I wrote it slowly.

From *My Silver Shoes*

Sissy: How old do you think I look, Joy?

Joy: You look old, Mum.

Sissy: Do you think I look as old as Teddy?

Joy: Teddy is seventeen years younger than you.

Sissy: But he looks older, doesn't he?

Joy: You look very well for your age but you are eighty.

Sissy: I don't think I look eighty, do you? Do I look all right?
  I don't have no future to talk about, do I? Do I look all right?

Joy: Yes, you look lovely, Mum.

This is my best work about the Muse. It shows her sweetness, her kindness, her generosity of spirit.

Then it snowed. And the boats had stopped for the winter.

Blow this! I'm going to Antigua to join Joan.

Josie went to stay in Antigua with Joan and Joan's daughter Kim, the potter.

Antigua
1984

My dear Nell,

Well my love I got here the flight wasn't so good, my heart went in my mouth a couple of times Kim and Joan met me, well love I'm shore you must of read Tobaco Road or seen Gone With the Wind, well that should give you a rough idea how I'm living I'm – in the olden days, Water on ration Nell your never believe it I was in cold water every day. No baths, and by the time you start the shower and you got the soap on you, the water run out.

Fuck me you would never believe it.

Kim has 4 cats 3 dogs, chicken ducks, Goat, rabbits and at the moment turtel which tomorrow has its head cut of to sell in the restrant. My room backs on to it so I have music until 12 o'clock at night drives me fucking mad. Joan said I'll get used to it. She deaf plus she got the room behind me.

Well besides that the place is beauful the beach are paridise – so blue white and green can't explain it.

You have to be so rich to live in the big houses here Oh Nell they are lovely we went to Mill Reaf, I explain what it was like, we spent the day there. I fantersized as I closed my eyes.

Most of the people were retered and terribly posh Oh what I would give to of stayed there. You just can't imagin, I'm not saying I'm not grateful to Kim & Joan, but I think I have been to spoilt in my time; I've never realy been a simple person, I like Luxury.

There's nothing to do here, but we go to the beach every day so slow, I know it will do me good.

We went to a place call half moon bay, that was lovely that's on the other side of the island, oh and there going to take me to St James hotel the best one I think on the island, To-night were going out

Oh Joan found herself a boy friend. He's bring a friend fuck noes what hes like he's got no chance, I don't think I can be bothered, in fact Nell they don't intrest me. How you been love and everyone send them my love.

That play you told me to write. I haven't started it yet, just cant get in the mood, I think if we go back to Mill Reaf it would come to me. I'm shore, haven't got the atmasfer here.

Well my love I'll write tomorrow and let you know how my night went so until tomorrow.

Well good morning my love here I am in a lovely hotel called 'Barmose' Kim & Joan are in the pool.

Well we had a terrific night out, met my date his name is James (not bad) we going out in a 4 some Monday night.

Well you never believe it but me & Joan have made some lovely vases. Kim given Joan top marks, me bottom mark as she said I rush to much. her work shop is lovely and she has lots of customers. You know your tiles you had for your Bath room she has a big order for them. Well I been here nearly a week, I fucking dread comeing home to the cold, I still have my cough.

But not smoking so much, isn't that good? How all the family? send them my love, Joan has packed up smoking. Well can you Imajin us all sitting here under the palm trees drinking on lovely Malabos (Pinocalata and rum punches.) Good. wish you were here my love it would be lovely.

Well my love no more to tell you will write again. Oh were going to Shirly Highs Hotel now so take care of yourself and come out soon.

Love Josie xxxx

*Josie and me,
and me and Joan
in Antigua*

So I flew out.

I joined them and we lived in a hut with fretwork windows and a fan and an outdoor shower.

At night a cool breeze blew through the fretwork bringing shadows of dancing branches and the smell of the sea.

Every morning Joan would bring us tea and biscuits in bed.

Nearby was an out-of-doors bar run by two transvestites and I'd go, still in my nightdress, and have a cold beer sitting on a stool in the early morning sun watching small boys playing cricket in the sand. Life couldn't get much better.

We sat on the beach. We painted each other's toenails. We drank cocktails from a thermos. We spoke of financial problems. We spoke of our love life. We spoke of husbands and sometimes we cried.

And at night we went dancing in the local bar and Josie lost her silver sandals and the next day she found them hanging, high up in a coconut palm.

Why do you love people?

It's hard to know if it really was because Josie had something so like my mother in both looks and character. A kind of freedom and generosity.

She, like my mother, had a fearless appetite for getting into scrapes.

She always did what she wanted. Just what she wanted and it often ended badly.

Lady Bird, Lady Bird, where have you been?

I was happy in her company.

What was it you liked about me, Josie?

She thought for a while. A long while.

You were something different.

Looking back on it, I think she loved me as an audience. She liked making me laugh. She loved me loving her.

I have been a writer ever since we met.

Notebook in my pocket.

Pencils in my bag.

'Wait! Hang on, Josie. You're going too fast. Slow down!'

And I'd pause her so I could write down her sylvan words and vivid thoughts that would sooner or later be used in whatever I was writing.

I just liked listening.

P.S. Maybe this explains something and maybe it doesn't.

This is what happened. It was 'before the war'.

My mother and father used to stay with friends at the weekends. These house parties were grand and they were invited to bring one child, my big sister, but I was left behind with Nanny.

On these rare occasions Nanny and I would go by train to stay with *her* mother.

Two days of happiness would begin. Me and Nanny. Nanny and me. (And Nanny's cheerful old mother.)

At teatime Nanny would bring a tray of tea into the sitting room.

Then I would sit on her knee while her mother poured out the tea.

I had to sit very still and be very good so nothing was spilt. I sat very still and I was very good and I drank my little cup of milky tea and ate my biscuit.

And then the war came and I was torn from Nanny's arms and put on a big ship to Canada.

No Nanny.

Many years went by. I was a grown-up with my own house. Josie brought her mother Sissy to tea.

I carried the teapot into the sitting room and put it on the table.

'Shall I pour?' said Sissy.

'Yes, please, Sissy.'

And she lifted the teapot and at that moment I felt a burning heat in my feet that rapidly travelled up my body so I was all on fire. A flame and at the same time a sensation of total bliss suffused my being, so all-encompassing that I thought they might notice but no, it was an invisible bliss. A silent ecstasy that spread through me – heat and light and a deep sense of pleasure. Josie and Sissy noticed nothing. Just drank their tea and were there.

Afterword

Now Josie is living on the south coast with a handsome man.

Their flat has a balcony with room for two chairs. Here she sits looking at the sea and remembering.

We talk most days.

Acknowledgements

Thank you Christie Hickman and
Thank you Mark Booth
For Huge Help

Also my dear friends John Cosgrove and Karin Grainger
who were often accosted in Kensington Gardens at 6 o'clock
in the morning to hear about *The Muse*.

Thank you to my agent, Alan Brodie and all his team

To Roddy Bloomfield for saying hallo.
Thanks to MacGibbon and Kee, and Amber Lane Press and
Bloomsbury for permission for extracts.

© Nell Dunn, 1967, *Poor Cow*, MacGibbon and Kee
© Nell Dunn, 1981, *Steaming*, Amber Lane Press
© Nell Dunn, 1996, *My Silver Shoes*, Bloomsbury Publishing Pc.

Picture credits:
pp 5,11, 16, 65, 79, 87, 139, 145: Collection of the author
pp 15, 31, 103: © Estate of Tina Tranter
p 129: Courtesy of STUDIOCANAL Films Ltd/ © Estate of
Tina Tranter

CENT 08-10-2020